A Female Apostle in Medieval Italy

THE MIDDLE AGES SERIES

Ruth Mazo Karras, Series Editor
Edward Peters, Founding Editor

A complete list of books in the series is available from
the publisher.

A FEMALE APOSTLE IN MEDIEVAL ITALY

The Life of Clare of Rimini

Jacques Dalarun, Sean L. Field,
and Valerio Cappozzo

PENN

UNIVERSITY OF PENNSYLVANIA PRESS

PHILADELPHIA

Published by
University of Pennsylvania Press
Philadelphia, Pennsylvania 19104-4112
www.upenn.edu/pennpress

Printed in the United States of America on acid-free paper
10 9 8 7 6 5 4 3 2 1

Hardcover ISBN: 978-1-5128-2303-5
Paperback ISBN: 978-1-5128-2304-2
eBook ISBN: 978-1-5128-2305-9

A Cataloging-in-Publication record for this book is
available from the Library of Congress.

CONTENTS

TIMELINE

1253: Death of Clare of Assisi

1254: Inquisition in the Romagna is entrusted to the Franciscans

1255: Canonization of Clare of Assisi

1257: Santa Maria in Trivio becomes the church of the Franciscans of Rimini, taking the name San Francesco

1259: Inquisition in the Romagna is divided between two Franciscan inquisitors, one in Faenza and one in Rimini

c. 1260: Birth of Clare of Rimini, daughter of Chiarello of Piero of Zacheo and his wife, Gaudiana

1282–1288: Malatesta of Verucchio is *podestà* of Rimini

c. 1282: Execution of Clare's father and brother

1288: Malatesta of Verucchio is driven out of Rimini by the Ghibelline party

1288–1306: The Clarissan nuns of Begno take refuge in Rimini

1290: Malatesta of Verucchio reclaims power in Rimini

1294–1303: Pontificate of Boniface VIII

1295: Malatesta of Verucchio solidifies his power in Rimini

c. 1295: Clare's surviving brother is exiled to Urbino; Clare joins him there

1299–1300:	Creation of a lay tribunal to assist the inquisitor in Rimini
1300:	Creation of a compilation for inquisitors using documents related to Rimini
1300:	Gherardo Segarelli is burned at Parma
1303–1305:	Dante's *On Vernacular Eloquence*
1305:	Death of Santuccia Carabotti of Gubbio
1305–1314:	Pontificate of Clement V
1306–1308:	Legation of Cardinal Napoleone Orsini in northern Italy
c. 1306:	Napoleone Orsini, passing through Rimini, meets Clare and gives her permission to have a cleric recite the office
1307:	Fra Dolcino and his companion Margherita are burned at Vercelli
c. 1307:	Dante begins *The Divine Comedy*
1308:	Earthquake at Rimini
1308–1319:	Frescoes at Sant'Agostino of Rimini are painted
1309:	Clement V settles the papacy at Avignon
1312:	Death of Malatesta of Verucchio
1312–1317:	Malatestino dell'Occhio governs Rimini
1314:	Dino of the Rossi family, Clare's relative, is *podestà* of Padua
1316–1334:	Pontificate of John XXII
1317:	John XXII condemns the *Fraticelli*
1317–1326:	Ferrantino and Pandolfo Malatesta govern Rimini
1318:	General chapter of the Order of the Augustinian Hermits meets at Rimini

1320–1321:	Dante completes *The Divine Comedy*
1321:	Death of Dante in Ravenna
1322:	Mention of "the church of Sister Clare" in a manuscript copied at Rimini for Ferrantino Malatesta
1323:	John XXII condemns the idea of the absolute poverty of Christ and the apostles
1323–1324:	Bernard Gui finishes his *Practice of the Inquisition*
1323–1328:	Girolamo Fisici is bishop of Rimini
1324–1329:	*The Life of the Blessed Clare of Rimini* is written. Death of Clare of Rimini.
1329:	First known testament that includes a bequest to "the sisters of Sister Clare" of Rimini
c. 1330:	Zanchino Ugolini writes his *Treatise on the Material of Heretics*
c. 1330:	First triptych created in honor of Clare of Rimini
1334:	Zanchino Ugolini participates in the revision of the communal statutes of Rimini
1335–1350:	Second triptych created in honor of Clare of Rimini
1450–1500:	Unique manuscript of *The Life of the Blessed Clare of Rimini* is copied
1522:	Santa Maria degli Angeli becomes a house of the Order of St. Clare
1751:	Cure of Sister Maria Vittoria at Santa Maria degli Angeli
1755:	Publication in Rome of Giuseppe Garampi's *Memorie ecclesiastiche appartenenti all'istoria e al culto della B. Chiara di Rimini*
1782–1784:	Beatification process for Clare of Rimini

1785:   Clare of Rimini proclaimed beatified by Pope Pius VI

1810:   Santa Maria degli Angeli is destroyed

c. 1943:   Clare of Rimini's remains are moved to the church of
                Corpolò

A Female Apostle in Medieval Italy

INTRODUCTION

The book you are about to read centers on a fascinating woman whose story is preserved in a fascinating text. The woman, Clare, was born in the Italian city of Rimini around 1260 and died there between 1324 and 1329. The Italian text, *La vita della beata Chiara da Rimino la quale fo exemplo a tucte le donne vane*, or *The Life of the Blessed Clare of Rimini Who Was an Example for All Vain Ladies*, was probably composed by a friar from the Franciscan house in Rimini, working closely with a group of Clare's spiritual daughters.

What is so remarkable about Clare and her *Life*? Just about everything. *The Life of the Blessed Clare of Rimini* is probably the earliest work of hagiography (saint's life) written directly in Italian, in an era when most such lives were still composed in Latin, the sacred language of the church. The first decades of the fourteenth century were exactly the period in which Italian emerged as a literary language. The most famous figure in this emergence, the Florentine Dante Alighieri (1265–1321), was a nearly exact contemporary of Clare's. When Dante died in Ravenna, only fifty-five kilometers (thirty-five miles) up the Adriatic coast from Rimini, he had just finished *The Divine Comedy*, his brilliant tour through the medieval cosmos and the Christian afterlife. If *The Life of the Blessed Clare of Rimini* is today considerably less well-known than Dante's masterwork, it nevertheless contributed to the same process of establishing Italian as a vehicle for exalted expression.

Our text is also one of the very few works of medieval hagiography to have been written before its subject's death (or, at least, so we will argue). Most saints' lives include elaborate scenes of the saint's last illness, followed by an all-important recounting of posthumous miracles that prove her or his sanctity. They are generally based on retrospective testimony, sometimes given many decades later. Clare's *Life*, by contrast, seems to have been begun during her last illness, while those who knew her best gathered around her in her last days. The result is a vivid work that tells the story of a controversial, uncompromising woman, set against the background of her roiling city, her star-crossed family, and the tumultuous political and religious landscape of her age.

Saints' lives are usually crafted as "success stories," often describing a perfect child who becomes a perfect adult, or a youthful sinner who converts to impeccable penitence. Clare's story does loosely fit the "sinner to saint" model. But rather than representing Clare as an edifying image of a docile holy woman, her hagiographer reveals all her scandals, her controversies, and her frustrations. Twice married, twice widowed, and twice exiled from her city, Clare eventually established herself as a penitent living in a little roofless cell in the ruins of the Roman walls of Rimini. She sought, at first, a life of solitary asceticism (self-denial) and holiness, praying and doing penance for her perceived sins. Her reception in Rimini, however, was not entirely welcoming. Her words and actions in the streets and squares of the city drew such vehement anger from local churchmen that she was denounced from the pulpit as a demonic danger to her neighbors. Yet she also gained the support of a Dominican bishop, a Franciscan-leaning cardinal, and some important inhabitants of Rimini, allowing her to establish a fledgling community of like-minded sisters. She traveled to Assisi and Venice, spoke out as a teacher and preacher (even if her hagiographer is careful never to use that word), but also suffered a revolt by her spiritual daughters.

As a rhetorical case for Clare's sanctity, *The Life of the Blessed Clare of Rimini* might be considered something perilously close to a failure; it presents a number of reasons *not* to canonize her! But as a historical document, it offers richly compelling testimony to the day-to-day details—the political conflicts, the social expectations, the trials and tribulations, and the exuberant joys—of life in a medieval Italian city.

Italy during Clare's lifetime experienced profound political strife and rapid religious change. There was no unified state of Italy in the Middle Ages. The southern kingdom of Naples (or just The Regno, "the kingdom") was ruled by a branch of the French royal family from the 1260s to 1282, and then fought over between French and Aragonese claimants through the rest of Clare's life. The rising power of the papacy dominated Rome and extended its influence across much of the central Italian peninsula. The popes' immediate presence had diminished, however, by 1309, when Pope Clement V moved to Avignon, on the Rhone north of the Alps, where the papal court remained until 1377, long after Clare's death. Northern Italy formed a patch-work of city-states, the most important of which were Milan, Florence, Ven-ice, and Genoa. Each had its own internal factions, and each plotted to gain the upper hand over its neighbors.

Medieval cities, especially Italian cities, with their rapid economic and cultural development, served as stages for civic performance and religious ritual. The city, its main square (*piazza*) and its streets, became the scene on which the hopes, protests, conflicts, and celebrations of an explosive society played out. A medieval Italian city such as Rimini in Clare's lifetime was a theater, a laboratory, and an incubator for change.

The dynamic new religious element in this landscape was the rise of the mendicant orders—most importantly, the Franciscans and Dominicans. The Italian Francis of Assisi (1181–1226) and the Castilian Dominic of Caleruega (1170–1221) founded new brotherhoods modeled on the lives of the apostles. These friars (or brothers) lived in poverty, traveled from town to town, and preached the Gospel in an effort to win souls for Christ. The Dominicans, or Preaching Brothers, were a highly educated clerical order dedicated to com-bating heresy. This background let Dominicans slip easily into the new of-fice of inquisitor of heretical depravity, created to suppress religious dissidence in the 1230s and increasingly organized in Italy from the 1250s onward. The Franciscans, or Lesser Brothers, were at first a group of less educated laymen, like their founder Francis, the son of a merchant from the Umbrian town of Assisi. But the Lesser Brothers, too, moved in the direction of clericalization and education, creating a long-simmering internal rift that had broken into open conflict between more moderate and more zealous ("spiritual") wings of the order by the end of the thirteenth century. Both orders eventually as-sumed important places in the nascent universities of Europe, producing some of the most important scholastic theologians of the age.

Women were drawn to the same apostolic ideals that animated Francis and Dominic. In this context, as was usually the case, the Franciscan scene produced the fiercest battles and the most controversial outcomes. The most famous woman associated with Francis and his movement was Clare of Assisi (1194–1253). She may first have hoped to live side by side with the friars, but quickly became the abbess of a settled group of "Poor Ladies" living outside Assisi. The papacy worked to turn a network of similar communities into a more traditional order, while Clare's tried to preserve her preferred life of radical poverty. After Clare of Assisi's death in 1253 and her canonization in 1255, the papacy created the Order of St. Clare in 1263 as the approved model for Franciscan nuns willing to live a monastic existence enclosed behind sturdy walls. But other women, in Italy and elsewhere, sought other ways of living out a mendicant life, inspired by Francis but uninterested in enclosure. As we encounter the world of Clare of Rimini, we will meet the examples of many of these women, such as Umiliana de' Cerchi (d. 1246), Rose of Viterbo (d. 1251), Margherita Colonna (d. 1280), Margherita of Cortona (d. 1297), Clare of Montefalco (d. 1308), Angela of Foligno (d. 1309), Umiltà of Faenza (d. 1310), and Michelina of Pesaro (d. 1356). The Italian cities of the thirteenth and fourteenth centuries were alive with possibilities for women's voices to be heard, but hardly devoid of danger for those who spoke too boldly.

* * *

The goal of this book is to let twenty-first-century readers enter Clare of Rimini's world, in all its excitement and with all its complexity. With this goal in mind, we have taken an unorthodox approach. A volume like this—centered on a medieval primary source translated into English for modern readers—usually begins with a thirty- or forty-page introduction and then moves on to the translated primary source itself. But *The Life of the Blessed Clare* is such an innovative text that we think it deserves an equally innovative treatment. So, rather than start with lengthy context and commentary, we dive right into Chapter 1 of the *Life* in English translation, adhering as closely as possible to the wording and flavor of the Italian, and then use the chapter as a springboard to address the issues that it raises. We repeat this pattern for the twelve chapters and an epilogue that make up the *Life*, exploring aspects of medieval society from political power to marriage and sexuality, from gender roles to religious change, from pilgrimage to urban structures, and from sanctity to heresy. In other words, rather than front-loading scholarly context and commentary, we allow the text itself to guide us (authors and readers alike) into a gradually deepening understanding of life in an Italian city around 1300. We give our hagiographer and his female informants room to explain the Italy of Dante and Giotto (the most famous painter of the age) at their own pace and with their own rhythms. Our job is to follow this lead and to proceed down the paths that the text pioneers. Let's start with a road map, to lay out in advance the *Life*'s basic structure and the most important questions it raises:

Chapter 1. Clare's family, her first exile, and her two marriages. How was a medieval Italian city governed, and what were the risks and rewards of elite political battles?

Chapter 2. Clare's conversion from luxurious marriage to penitent celibacy. How did earthly and spiritual loves relate to each other in medieval mentalities?

Chapter 3. Clare's penitent practices. How did harsh asceticism take on meaning in the medieval worldview?

Chapter 4. Clare's new exile from Rimini and her first steps toward an independent religious life. How did medieval women's bodily actions mark out spiritual relationships?

Chapter 5. Clare's return to Rimini and her move to a cell within the city walls. How could the speech of an urban recluse be heard at the center of the spiritual and charitable networks that animate a medieval city?

Chapter 6. Clare's brush with heresy. How did inquisitors construct heresy and orthodoxy as mirror images of each other?

Chapter 7. Clare's apostolic mission to convert those around her. How could a medieval woman teach publicly amid controversies over poverty and obedience?

Chapter 8. Clare's growing community. How could a woman dedicated to poverty and penance make the practical moves necessary to purchase a dwelling and impose her will?

Chapter 9. Clare's public performances and interaction with a powerful cardinal of the church. How could local politicians and princes of the church envision holy women as political assets?

Chapter 10. Clare's pilgrimage to Assisi. How were medieval women able to travel and form networks across the roads of Italy?

Chapter 11. Clare's visions. How did art and visions construct and reflect each other in medieval visual culture?

Chapter 12. Clare's battles with demons and her last days. How could a language of sexuality express medieval spirituality?

Epilogue. Clare's death, the composition of her *Life*, and the construction of her cult. How does a medieval text reach the modern world?

Each chapter, in fact, does more than just raise a question: it poses a challenge—a challenge in Clare's life and a challenge for anyone eager to understand the complexity of such an experience.

The reader may, of course, choose to focus on the translated *Life* first, and to return to the modern commentary later. Or the reader might focus only on chapters and commentary that address issues of particular interest. But careful attention to the entire text will allow patterns of meaning to emerge, as connections build chapter by chapter and paragraph by paragraph. For certain crucial questions, answers slowly take shape only as the reader progresses: Who wrote the *Life*? When and why? Where did the information come from? Why is the text written in the vernacular? What was the relationship of the author(s) to Clare? How did the text survive through the centuries? And to all of these: How do we know? In addressing these questions, we rarely have much to go on, beyond what the text tells us, so they can be answered only by very careful scrutiny of the *Life*. Reading closely with these questions in mind opens the same process of discovery that makes medieval scholarship so exciting for specialists.

In sum, this book offers the progressive unearthing of a society, its hierarchies, its codes, its beliefs, its tensions, and its conflicts, as seen through Clare of Rimini's life and the *Life*. In one sense, our less-than-linear approach is akin to the way medieval scholars liked to work. In the universities that had developed by 1200 in cities like Bologna (115 kilometers [seventy miles] northwest of Rimini), scholars would copy in the center of the page an authoritative text, such as a biblical passage or an edict of canon law, and then compose their commentary around it. Like these early scholars, we think it essential to place the source text in front of readers' eyes as we offer interpretations or expositions. Yet from another angle, our approach reflects the twenty-first-century reading habits of the digital universe, where we so often find ourselves with multiple browser windows open on a laptop or scrolling through one thread of comments after another on our phones. Reading is not always left to right and top to bottom; discovery is not always along a straight path. Perhaps, in certain ways, the medieval and modern worlds are not so far apart after all.

Without further delay, let us turn to the text as it takes Clare through the crowded streets of Rimini, on her journeys to Urbino, Assisi, and Venice, and back to her battles for an uncompromising life in the heart of her city.

In la bella, fertile et, in mare et terra, notissima città de Arimino de la magnifica italica provincia de Romagnia, de nobile et generosa famiglia de mesere Chiarello de Piero de Zacheo, patre, et madonna Gaudiana, matre, in li anni del Signore M°CCC° o circa, una figliola nacque per nome Chiara . . .

CHAPTER 1

Space, Time, Social Setting

1. In the beautiful and fertile city of Rimini,[1] famous on land and sea, in the magnificent Italian province of Romagna,[2] from the noble and generous family of Sir Chiarello of Piero of Zacheo, her father, and of Lady Gaudiana, her mother,[3] around the year of the Lord 1300[4] was born a little girl named Clare, of clear and holy hope, as was later revealed by the benevolence of the highest God. This creature blessed by God was seven years old when her dear mother, passing over to the next life, rendered her soul to God, while Clare remained with her father and two brothers. So her father remained a widower until Clare reached the age of ten.[5] Then, taken and overcome by love, he entered a second marriage with another wife and joined himself to this lady, who was full of all goodness and virtue. And to her young son, he gave his daughter Clare to be his wife. [Clare's husband] lived with her with pleasure and happiness, but finally he was taken by death at a young age, leaving behind his beautiful and dear partner. And shortly afterward, the lady who had been Clare's stepmother also died.

2. At this time, as it happens in many particular places, conflict and strife broke out in the city [of Rimini]. In the ensuing upheaval, Chiarello, one of the city patricians, was chased from his sweet homeland and deprived of the goods from his house and elsewhere. Clare, now growing in years and of extreme physical beauty, full of lasciviousness and putting off all love of God, reached the age of twenty-four, very gentle and beautiful.[6] There a certain reconciliation came about between the principal men of Rimini, through which her father, her brothers, and she were restored to their homeland. But this was an evil fortune

and an unhappy day because shortly afterward, her father and a brother were decapitated.[7] Still, for all that, Lady Clare did not neglect her blameworthy style and her vain and lascivious and ornate manners; she was wrapped in all error and vanity, as though blind to her dishonest actions and the evil desires of her heart, led astray from all light and the path of virtues. And in this lasciviousness, she took another husband, whom she had loved and desired beyond all good reason. She was inflamed in his love not only because she was pleased by him but also because he was rich in wealth and other resources and powerful in the homeland of Rimini. With this husband, she was much given to vanity in clothing, speech, and gestures. And especially given to pleasures of the mouth, she refused no foods that she judged worthy of gluttony; and [there were no foods] that she did not want, by delight of eating as well as drinking, abandoning all the delicacy expected of a lady. Her husband also grew soft in this gluttony. And in this disordered existence, she lived until her thirty-fourth year, vain, luxurious, and disordered.[8]

*   *   *

Right from the start, the text is rooted in space, time, and social context. The date of Clare's birth, given here as "around 1300," is the least significant of these elements for our hagiographer. In fact, the date should be about 1260 (it's possible that the mistake results from a later scribe miscopying roman numerals). Geographic space is more carefully delineated. Clare's world is the Italian peninsula—more precisely, the "magnificent" region of Romagna in the northeast and, specifically, the "beautiful and fertile" city of Rimini by the Adriatic Sea (see Map 1). Although Italy was not a political entity before the nineteenth century, the idea of "Italian" culture, language, and inheritance resonated powerfully in the age of Dante. The Romagna centered on Ravenna, where the Byzantine or "Roman" emperors maintained a strong presence up through the eighth century CE. Rimini itself had been founded in the third century BCE at the spot where the river for which it was named, the Ariminus, reached the Adriatic. Following the Roman period, the city fell successively under the sway of Gothic leaders, Frankish kings, and Roman popes; but by the twelfth century, it was loosely under the dominion of the

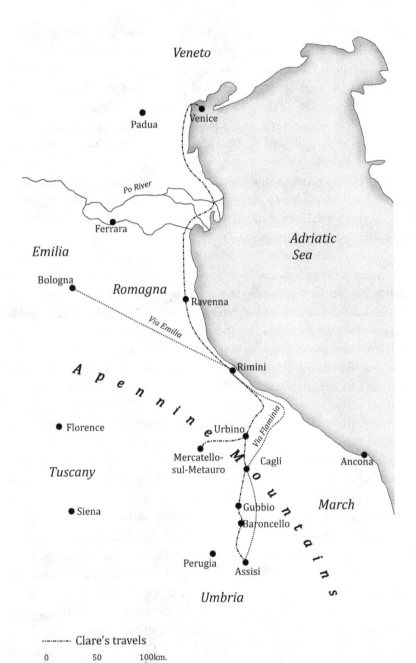

Veneto

Padua

Venice

Po River

Ferrara

Emilia

Adriatic
Sea

Bologna

Romagna

Ravenna

Via Emilia

Rimini

Apennine

Florence

Urbino

Via Flaminia

Tuscany

Mercatello-
sul-Metauro

Cagli

Ancona

Siena

Mountains

Gubbio

March

Baroncello

Perugia

Assisi

Umbria

-------- Clare's travels

0   50   100km.

Map 1. Clare's Travels. © M. Cecilia Gaposchkin.

German, or Holy Roman, emperor. Like other cities of the region, taking advantage of papal-imperial disputes, Rimini took shape in this period as a commune (Italian: *comune*): a nearly autonomous city governed by various councils and magistrates and asserting its power over the surrounding countryside (the *contado*). By 1200, the city had 15,000 to 20,000 inhabitants; during the thirteenth century, its institutions of self-government grew more complex, with the appointment of a *podestà* (an outsider chosen from another town to direct the city for a limited period). Like most Italian cities, it was riven by clashes between rival clans; between Guelfs (the party of the pope) and Ghibellines (the party of the emperor); and between the aristocracy on one hand, the wealthy but non-noble merchants, bankers, and lawyers (the *popolo grasso*) on the other, and finally the craftsmen, shopkeepers, and laborers (the *popolo minuto*).

The *Life* clearly places Lady (*madonna*) Clare in the upper echelons of this society, in a "noble and generous family." It's true that in hagiographic sources, an allusion to the saint's "noble" birth can be a meaningless platitude. But in this case, the claim is verifiable. We don't know anything about Clare's father, Chiarello, beyond what we read in the *Life*; he was "one of the city patricians" (urban nobles) and possessed goods inside and outside Rimini. But we will meet (in Chapter 5) a certain "Sir Dino of the Rossi family, who was [Clare's] relative." This man would become *podestà* of Padua in 1314, was referred to as a nobleman in his testament, and is given the title "Sir" (*messere*) in the text. His noble status is further proved by the fact that his sister married Malatestino dell'Occhio, from the powerful Malatesta family, which was in the process of imposing its dominance on Rimini. As a "relative" of Sir Dino de' Rossi and as the daughter of Sir (*messere*) Chiarello of Piero of Zacheo and Lady (*madonna*) Gaudiana, Clare was decidedly well-born.

The scene has been set, and the story can begin. After losing her mother at age seven, around 1267, Clare lives with her father and two brothers. Three years later, her father remarries. Eventually, Clare is given in marriage to her new stepmother's son. Although the medieval church upheld an expansive definition of incest, this marriage does not seem to have been regarded as technically taboo. Still, it may have carried a whiff of scandal. Perhaps there is a suggestion of divine punishment in the way Clare's stepmother and husband are quickly carried off by death. In the early 1280s, in a new round of civic unrest in Rimini, Sir Chiarello finds himself on the losing side and suffers exile with his children. When peace is made, around 1284, they return. But scores remain to be settled, and Chiarello and one of his sons are quickly executed. As the hagiographer stresses, this sort of reversal of fortune was all too common in the turbulent Italian communes of the day (even if decapitation was less so). The family's exile and return must have occurred following the Guelf Malatesta of Verucchio's installation as *podestà* in 1282. Clare's family evidently adhered to the Ghibelline cause, as shown by the fact that her remaining brother was later (see Chapter 4) exiled to Urbino, a traditional place of refuge for Rimini's Ghibellines. Clare's family had decidedly chosen the wrong side. For one thing, it was somewhat awkward, in retrospect, to have a prospective saint ranged with the imperial party against the pope's partisans. Still, this was a minor matter in light of the endlessly shifting alliances and chaotic enmities that characterized local Italian politics. Far more weighty was the simple fact of having ended up on the losing side. Clare's father and brother paid for this miscalculation with their lives. If Italian politics were topsy-turvy, they were far from benign.

When Clare and her family made their ill-fated return to Rimini (around 1284, when she was twenty-four), it was to a city now solidly dominated by the Malatesta clan. The roots of this hardheaded family lay in Verucchio, sixteen kilometers (ten miles) outside Rimini, but several members of the family were citizens of Rimini by 1216. In 1239, Malatesta della Penna became *podestà* of the city. The second half of the century was marked by battles between his son Malatesta of Verucchio—whom Dante (*Inferno* XXVII, 46–48) would call the "old mastiff"—and the Ghibelline party. Malatesta of Verucchio seized power and maintained his hold on the position of *podestà* from 1282 to 1288, monopolizing an office intended to be held for a short period by someone from outside the city and hence above local factions. In 1288, he and his followers were chased out of the city; in 1290, he returned. In 1295, Malatesta of Verucchio defeated all rivals (this was when Clare and her surviving brother would have to flee to Urbino), and from this point ruled without serious opposition, until his death in 1312. For all practical purposes, the commune was at an end, giving way to an era of familial lordship. Malatesta rule in Rimini continued with Malatestino dell'Occhio (Dante's "new mastiff") up to 1317, after which his son Ferrantino governed jointly with his uncle Pandolfo. With the popes absent from Italy after 1305 (settled in Avignon from 1309 to 1378), the traditional Guelf allegiance to the papacy meant less, and the Malatesta spread their power over neighboring cities.

This was the civic context that Clare faced after 1284. Her personal religious conversion would be, in part, the reaction of a woman navigating the complexities of a profound political reversal and its disastrous consequences for her family.

CHAPTER 2

From Human Desire to Divine Love

3. While Clare was living in great satisfaction with her beloved husband and her ornate clothing, enjoying all kinds of delicate foods, the clarity of God began to shine in Clare, and to lift all blindness and darkness of her heart and mind.[1] So much that one day when she entered the church of the Lesser Brothers,[2] it seemed that a creature said to her, "Force yourself, Clare, to say an 'Our Father' in praise and memory of God, and to think of nothing else!" She seemed to take much pleasure from this, but she could not explain from her own understanding what this vision was. And advancing in age, she felt in herself an inestimable pleasure growing in her heart. She never failed, if a stronger wind blew in the air,[3] to leave her house and then, with an unbelievable sweetness, to visit alone orchards and gardens. In shadowy places and on clear riverbanks, she would lie down and rest, with a light and satisfied mind. Her family circle would say to her, "All the other ladies suffering from melancholy flee from loneliness; ours searches these things out and delights in them with all happiness!" These women did not know that, already, a little ray of divine grace had begun to warm and illuminate her.

4. Once, when visiting the church of the seraphic Francis,[4] and not without some sweet thoughts of God, the glorious Virgin Mary appeared to her (not visible to others of her company but only to her), surrounded by many angels, and she said to her: "What good, Clare, did abundant riches, the flowering of fine youth, the continuous assistance of doctors, nobility of family, superb possessions, and youthful boasting do for your husband, who was separated from you by a little fever,

passing away to the next life?" By this voice, by these stupefying words that penetrated her heart, her breast, and her inner being, that separated her from all love of the world and inflamed her with the love of God, Lady Clare was suddenly transformed into having another will, different from the one she had had before, as though she had taken on new thoughts and a new body. She placed all her desire in God; in God, she anchored her faith, love, and hope;[5] for God, who is our highest good, she wanted to spend the rest of her time, having decided to recognize and emend her past errors, intending to repose tearfully in the Crucified One alone. And abandoning worldly desires, she was confirmed in her intention to live with Christ. With this firm disposition, with her pious prayers obtaining the consent of her husband in the flesh, she took on a religious habit and clothing.[6] And she dedicated herself to celestial things with such spiritual care and attention that after the death of her second husband, with whom she had stayed for about twelve years (and she was then thirty-four years old),[7] freed from marriage and made a religious woman, renouncing all terrestrial thoughts, she chose the Son of the Virgin[8] for her spouse, to whom she entirely pledged herself. Clare, in true clarity,[9] was made worthy of such a gift from the celestial throne, in the eternal memory of Rimini. For this, as for all other things, may God be blessed in eternity!

*   *   *

One by one, Clare had lost her mother, her husband, her stepmother, her father, and one of her brothers. Finding herself suddenly without family protection, she could have sought refuge in a convent. But desire pushed her to marry again, to a man who was not only good-looking but rich and powerful. For a decade, up to the age of thirty-four (around 1294), she enjoyed the pleasures of flesh and food with this like-minded husband. It's true that medieval marriages were often arranged and made for economic reasons, particularly within elite families. Indeed, Clare's first marriage had evidently been decided upon by her father, when she was still quite young. But Clare chose this second marriage freely ("she took another husband"), for love and out of a desire for sexual satisfaction and a luxurious life.

For our hagiographer, however, nature and good morals are subverted by a mature woman seeking out a marriage partner in her "vain" desire for pleasure. Moreover, our author castigates Clare's enjoyment of all kinds of luxury. Clare's second husband is rich and able to provide fine clothes and delicious foods, as well as physical pleasures. But in the *Life*, all this earthly husband's glittering attributes serve only to heighten the hagiographer's lesson: no terrestrial marriage can compare to union with Christ, the heavenly husband. The Virgin Mary's admonition reveals that Clare's first husband had likewise possessed "nobility of family"; but what good had his youth, money, nobility, or pride done for either of them, since death had so easily and so quickly snatched him away?

Married women were rarely regarded as possible saints. The church fathers taught that, at best, a dutiful wife might receive a thirtyfold reward in heaven, while the reward for chaste widows would be sixtyfold, and for virgins a hundredfold. The early fathers, such as St. Jerome, exhibited a near-obsessional disgust for human sexuality. As a result, they placed the ideal of virginity on a pinnacle, particularly for women. In the early Middle Ages, from the sixth through the tenth centuries—when the Merovingian and Carolingian dynasties ruled the kingdom of the Franks and the Ottonians eventually came to dominate the German Empire—noble and royal wives enjoyed a certain access to power, and some of them did indeed acquire reputations for sanctity. This recognition of powerful women's potential sanctity was probably due not to any Germanic tradition of respect for women but to the political realities of an age when elite families controlled ecclesiastical and monastic institutions as well as political offices, so that wives and mothers might be venerated as influential religious patrons or abbesses. But the eleventh century saw a revolutionary reform movement within the church, known as the Gregorian Reform (after Pope Gregory VII). As part of a wider drive to separate the church from the impurities of secular society, the reformers insisted on celibacy for priests and other clerics. In this context, the ideal of virginity weighed ever more heavily on women. The reformer Peter Damian (d. 1072), for example, echoed Jerome in arguing that divine omnipotence knew only one limit: God cannot restore virginity to someone who has lost it. In the thirteenth and fourteenth centuries, however, the doorway to sanctity slowly began to crack open for married women, especially in Italy. Clare slips in here, following trails blazed in hagiographic works.

Hagiographic tradition effectively offered two paths to a married woman. On the one hand, she could begin by wallowing in the sinful sexual pleasures of marriage, but then undergo an abrupt shock of conversion, turning away from the world. The Bible offered several models for this kind of female repentance—above all, the sinner who bathed the Lord's feet with her tears, generally conflated with Mary Magdalene by western European Christians. On the other hand, a woman could be forced into marriage against her will, share her husband's bed only with a sense of resignation or (better yet) disgust, and eventually persuade her husband to allow her to live chastely, either within marriage or by retreating to a religious life as a sort of consolation prize for her lost virginity. A famous example of this type was St. Radegund, the captured Thuringian princess who was forced to marry the Merovingian king Clothar but who eventually succeeded in freeing herself from marriage and retired to the monastery of Sainte-Croix in Poitiers, where she died in 587.

Saintly Italian women of the thirteenth and fourteenth centuries—those who were not virgins—followed one of these two paths. Margherita of Cortona (d. 1297), for example, lived for nine years as the mistress of a dissolute nobleman. When he was mysteriously assassinated, the sight of his corpse inspired Margherita to turn away from a life of pleasure. Angela of Foligno (d. 1309) similarly lived the high life in marriage before turning toward the Franciscans. Michelina of Pesaro (d. 1356), according to her later legend, was freed by the death of her spouse to enter the Franciscan Third Order, as the Holy Spirit urged her to do. On the other hand, we have the wives-in-spite-of-themselves. Umiliana de' Cerchi (d. 1246), who was forced to marry a rich usurer at age sixteen, lived as edifying a life as possible for five years, until her husband obligingly died. Umiltà of Faenza (d. 1310) dreamed of entering a monastery but had to marry the nobleman Ugolotto de' Caccianemici. The union ran into trouble when the husband's doctors advised that his health required chastity; eventually, both spouses entered the religious life.

The Life of the Blessed Clare combines the two paths. In the Franciscan church of Rimini, Clare hears a voice urging her to think only of praising God. The experience seems to produce an odd, melancholy effect as Clare meditates on it, even if "she could not explain" exactly what it meant. She takes to wandering alone, in the fresh air, among trees and flowers. The modest enclosed space of the garden stands in for the monastic desert, as a safe retreat that a woman could make without too much risk. Our author waxes poetic, picturing Clare emerging from the shadows to lie down near a sun-dappled riverbank, like the heroine of a medieval romance or a figure painted in the fresh colors of a tableau from the age of Giotto (who was said to have worked on the Franciscan church of Rimini), with a "little ray of light" to warm her. From the role of the wife sunk in luxury, Clare is now gradually adopting the pose of the wife-in-spite-of-herself. But the church of St. Francis draws her back, like a magnet. The Virgin appears, surrounded by angels but visible only to Clare. Mary abruptly reminds her (as we have just seen) how little the wealth and nobility of Clare's first husband could protect him from death. The shock completes Clare's conversion. She is "separated" from the world, mentally, spiritually, and physically. She has a "new will," determined to make amends for her past.

A conversion, however, is not a denial. Love and desire are not rejected, but redirected and reversed. "Love of the world" becomes "love of God." It is as though Clare has not only a new will but even a "new body." She is still "inflamed" with love, but with love directed now toward God. She lives a certain time in this liminal state, still married to an earthly husband but having received his permission to adopt religious dress and "live with Christ." At last, her husband's death allows her to take the final step, as St. Radegund did before her: not to live outside marriage but to be married for a third time—to the "Son of the Virgin," whom she now takes as her "spouse."

CHAPTER 3

Doing Penance

5. Sister Clare,[1] knowing that it was difficult for those who had grown up in sin to convert to God, and doubting the repentance of those who wait to repent until the very end of their lives, grieving for the sins that she had committed, confided that with the grace of her chosen spouse, Jesus Christ, she would not sin again in the future. Indeed, illuminated within by the strength of the Holy Spirit, she put all her thoughts, care, and effort into doing penance, awaiting the word of Christ in the Gospel: *Do penance and the kingdom of heaven* will arrive in you,[2] and especially the word of John the Baptist, *Behold the Lamb of God, behold him who takes away the sin of the world!*[3]

6. The true servant of God trod the land barefoot whenever she had to walk. And she did this for the love of our Lord Jesus Christ, who for love of us did not blush to hang naked on the cross.[4] For according to Holy Scripture, the affections of the mind are accustomed to show forth through the feet;[5] in fact, visibly suffering feet show that inside, invisibly and spiritually, goodness prevails, and that the power of God governs within, preserving the body from all stain and crime, just as the soles of the feet must be kept well washed and clean of all dust.[6] Not only did it seem good to the servant of God, Sister Clare, to walk shoeless, but with her flesh crucified within by sharp torments, she clothed herself in gray and beige cloth, so that she was not vexed and not thought to be proud because of the pomp and glory of fine clothing or velour, since those who adorn themselves with delicate clothing are not praised by God. She wore at her neck not a necklace of jewels or pearls but a little circle of iron, and the same on both arms

and her two knees. Her camisole was not made of fine, thin white linen, but it was a cuirass of heavy rusted iron, weighing about thirty pounds.[7] Over this, however, she wore white clothing, just as the other sisters were accustomed to wear.[8] And her bed was not made of soft light feathers but of hard boards, on which, tired and conquered by sleep, she would sometimes lie down.

7. Her delicate foods, with which she sustained a body tormented by penitence, were not the delicate meats for which the mouth usually waters; not hens, delicious boiled or roasted game, meat pies, or consommés. Nothing except bread alone, with pure water, was keeping her body fed and satisfied—and of these, not even enough to keep the body replenished; rather, she discarded part, as long as nature and life were sustained. She survived about eighteen years in such abstinence,[9] always content to eat and drink in this manner. She added nothing, if not sometimes what the charity of her companions and the little sisters (*sorelle*) of the monastery forced her to do. Then, so as not to seem to impose austerities and afflictions beyond all human measure, she would take a few mouthfuls of beans and touch her mouth to a cup, swallowing little or nothing. And this continued for perhaps three years. At the beginning of her conversion, during Easter feasts and on Sundays, she would pour a little olive oil on her food; but at other times, nothing. During the major Lent, from beginning to end, she would limit herself to uncooked herbs, giving up the *bread* that comforts and restores man's heart, *strengthens him*, and gives him joy.[10]

8. She began to torment her body beyond all measure and to diminish her usual strength, since it seemed to her possible to sustain life without the help of bread and wine. It was then that the Enemy of humankind began to tempt her severely, concerning such a renunciation of bodily nourishment and delicate way of life. She could not rid herself of this temptation through prayer, or flee it in any way. And when, on the verge of being conquered, she wanted to give in to the temptation and thought of consenting to everything, the demon began to mock her and to rejoice in having overcome her. But Jesus Christ, who always comes to the aid of his faithful and devout, came to support his servant Clare. Not permitting that she be further

tempted, and bringing her his favor, he intoned in her ears so that she said, "Arise for me, Christ, and help me![11] Come to me, you who are the guardian of men, the *root of David*, Hallelujah!"[12] Miraculous to say, at the sound of these words, she recovered such strength and vigor that she entirely overcame all the temptation. And then, inebriated with the Holy Spirit, at sunrise, she left her cell[13] and called a female companion, commanding that she prepare the embers. And after sending her [companion] away, she went in search of a toad; having divided it into four parts and roasted it—which is horrible to say!— she placed the venomous animal in her mouth and began to chew it with her lips, saying, "You glutton, swallow this delicate food and eat it!" And from this moment on, such demonic temptation ceased for her, and never again did the demon dare to tempt her with gluttony. Let anyone vowed and inclined to divine love [find] patience and hope in this example, because God works greatly in it for good, and makes all that is hard and terrible *light* and *sweet*;[14] but if, by chance, the lover rejects the effort and fear, that is not true love.

9. But let us return to the frugality and abstinence that the servant of God showed in her consumption of food. Fasting during the Lent of St. Martin[15] and that of Epiphany[16]—commencing on that date and continuing for forty days, as the Lord consecrated it with his most holy fast[17]—and for fifteen days before Pentecost and fifteen days before Ascension,[18] and on the vigils of the apostles and of St. John the Baptist,[19] and all the Saturdays throughout the year, she ate no fruit and no beans soaked in water, always keeping in mind the fast that the Lord left as an example for us.[20]

10. In sleeping habits, the rigor to which she held herself is also evident. During the major Lent, in the wall of the ancient city,[21] she would stand on her feet all night, so that she could not sleep at all. Neither cold nor rain nor any other bad weather could shake her from such an austere life. Sometimes, when she was afflicted like this, she would tie a rag[22] on her head and say, "Lord Jesus Christ, who came into this world from the breast of the Father for us sinners, to save us from sin[23]—and I know that it is not for the just but for the delinquent that you wanted to inhabit the earth![24]—hear me and grant my wish, my Lord, my God, me a sinner, guilty, unworthy, negligent, hateful

and evil!" Then she would say the entire Credo and more than a hundred times the Our Father, with a great abundance of tears, crying, "O
my evil soul, what great offense you have given to Christ by continuing
to sin!" Then, with great sighs from the heart, she would say, with effort, "Have mercy, God, on me, a sinner who has erred endlessly! In
you I hope, my Lord,[25] you who have redeemed me with your precious
blood." Then, sighing and crying with more force and intensity, she
would say, "My Lord, why and for whom were you tortured on the
gallows of the cross and did you spill your precious blood?"[26] And in
this austere denial of sleep, she lived continuously for nearly thirty
years.[27] And many times, from the octave of the Nativity of Our Lord[28]
right up to Easter, she would ceaselessly praise God. When, with divine
grace, she had already reached the age of sixty,[29] as far as the sisters
and little sisters (*sore et sorelle*) knew, the latter, fearing that the servant
of God would falter due to extreme and too arduous penance, tried
to stop her in order to calm her, but they could not.

11. And to briefly conclude this chapter on her harsh penance, as
much as the servant of God had enjoyed vain delights before her conversion, so much more she wanted to endure afflictions and penances
and to dedicate them to her Lord God.

*   *   *

"Do penance and the Kingdom of Heaven will arrive in you!" This is
Clare's cry. Now, before it is too late, she will repent of her past sins. But her
biblically based phrase is slightly jarring. In the book of Matthew, Jesus ex-
horts his followers to "Do penance, for the Kingdom of Heaven is at hand!"
We shall return (in Chapter 6) to the ways in which this seemingly minor
shift might have disconcerted potential critics.

Our hagiographer is usually precise with his terminology. Describing
Clare in her youth, he calls her simply Clare (*Chiara*). In her married life, he
refers to her as "Lady Clare" (*donna* or *madonna Chiara*). But the moment
she adopts a religious mode of life, she becomes "Sister Clare" (*sora Chiara*)
or "the servant of God." At the same time, our author refuses to recklessly
employ the vocabulary of sanctity. Only four times in the entire *Life* does he
refer to Clare as "blessed." He never calls her "St. Clare," only applying the

adjective "saintly" or "holy" to her "saintly life," or, at most, calling her a "saintly woman." Since the end of the twelfth century, the papacy had monopolized the formal power of canonization—the power to create a saint—and the process required a long investigation, detailed gathering of testimony, and sustained backing from powerful interests such as a royal family or a monastic order. A local author could hope to spark such a process, but overeager assertions of sanctity could easily backfire.

The hagiographer is also careful not to describe Clare's religious experience using terms that might evoke suspicion: he does not call her a beguine, anchoress, or recluse. But he is equally careful not to give her a more formal canonical status: she is never called a nun, a tertiary, or even a penitent. The author is well aware that Clare has no claim to any of these labels. She is certainly not a nun; she has not joined a recognized community, passed through a novitiate, or taken vows. No rule places her under a hierarchical authority that would guide her steps to salvation. Neither is she a tertiary. These were laymen and laywomen, often married, who combined the goals of the Gospels with a life in the world, promising sexual continence while devoting themselves to fasts, prayers, and works of charity. They were associated with the new mendicant orders of the thirteenth century—most importantly, the Franciscans (the *Fratres Minores*, or Lesser Brothers) and Dominicans (the *Fratres Praedicatores*, or Preaching Brothers). The designation "tertiaries" rested on the idea that the movements begun by St. Francis (d. 1226) and St. Dominic (d. 1221) included "first" orders of the male friars, "second" orders of vowed nuns, and "third" orders (chronologically last to come into existence) made up of laypeople under the spiritual care of the first order's priests.

We have already seen indications that the Franciscan Order might hold special significance for Clare: in Chapter 2, it was while visiting "the church of the Lesser Brothers," referred to again as "the church of the seraphic Francis," that she experienced her visions. Chapter 3 now provides further evidence of our text's Franciscan ties. Referring to Clare's habit of fasting during the Lents of St. Martin and Epiphany, our hagiographer describes them as "commencing on that date and continuing for forty days, as the Lord consecrated it with his most holy fast." The phrase comes directly from the Rule of the Lesser Brothers (*Regula bullata*). The author of the *Life* has intended to remain anonymous, but here he inadvertently gives us a clue as to his identity.

Only a member of Francis's order would have repeated this phrase word for word. Our hagiographer was almost certainly a Franciscan friar, a member of the community of St. Francis that had been installed in Rimini since 1257.

As for the term "penitent," it could refer broadly to a spiritual state. In that sense, Clare was indeed a penitent. But the word more precisely designated a canonical status, regulated by a consecration ceremony, specific rules, and ecclesiastical supervision. Tertiaries were really just one kind of penitent. The entry into the formal category of penitent, with its renunciation of worldly values, was marked by a ceremony that included a solemn promise and the adopting of a distinct mode of dress with the approval of an ecclesiastical authority, usually the local bishop. Those who sought an even more dramatic form of penitence could embrace the life of an anchoress or a recluse, a kind of voluntary burial-for-life in an urban cell that was often adjacent to a church. The *Lives* of Rose of Viterbo (d. 1251) and Umiltà of Faenza offer vivid examples of the solemn rituals that marked the transition to such a state. But there is nothing like this in Clare's case—just an interior journey, a conversion of the heart, that transforms Lady Clare into Sister Clare. The hagiographer's careful terminology balances the boldness of Clare's path.

Nothing constrains Clare's spirit. But to do penance is to impose painful denials and determined punishments on the body, following a tradition that originated in the deserts of Egypt in late antiquity. After Christianity had been adopted as the official religion of the Roman Empire, by the fourth century CE, a new breed of ascetics sought to equal the exploits of the early Christian martyrs who had suffered for the faith, and of Christ's own suffering on the cross, by inflicting physical punishments on their bodies. In this mode, Clare continually goes barefoot "with her flesh crucified within by sharp torments," for love of Christ, who hung "naked on the cross." The Crucifixion is not a metaphor to Clare; it is an object of obsessive imitation, and St. Jerome's exhortation "to follow naked the naked Christ" was particularly popular in Franciscan circles. Having given up her jewels, she now wears iron circles on her neck, arms, and knees; having discarded her fine linen undergarments, she wears a rusted iron casing, like a knight's cuirass, under her simple white clothing. When she seeks a little rest, she lies down not on soft pillows but on hard wooden boards. But even that is too easy—for three decades, so we are told, she preferred to stand and pray all night in the cold and the rain, begging for mercy and recalling Christ bleeding on the cross. Clare punishes her body and she suffers, but she suffers in imitation of Christ. When her body was exhumed in the seventeenth century, it was found encased in iron, exactly as the *Life* described.

We cannot impose modern mental categories on these medieval practices. It is impossible, and pointless, to imagine ourselves as Sigmund Freud diagnosing medieval people at a distance of seven centuries. Clare's ascetic practices are not pathologies. They are collective and codified behaviors. They have a certain ritual quality. Radegund, the Merovingian queen, had already mortified her royal flesh under a cilice, iron bands, and chains. Braided out of horsehair or a similar coarse material, the cilice (or hair shirt) transformed the penitent's skin into a fiery, itching mass of irritation. But it had to remain hidden under unassuming outer garments, so that the ascetic endured a secret martyrdom without receiving the least credit for her suffering. Italian hermits of the eleventh century had specialized in a similar kind of ascetic cuirass, which bit into the flesh at every movement. Dominic "of the iron cuirass" (d. 1060) is a prime example. According to Peter Damian, the reforming cardinal who wrote his *Life*, this Dominic also invented the practice of "the discipline"—that is, self-flagellation with leather whips, iron chains, or biting cords tipped with nails.

Penitence was a competition. It is hard for us to understand this today. But seven hundred years from now, who will understand the apparently pointless sufferings of a champion triathlete? Who will grasp the delirious joy of the man or woman who crosses the finish line of the Boston Marathon first, and then collapses in exhilarated exhaustion? Suffering for a sporting event does not strike us as abnormal, precisely because it is a collective and consensual abnormality in our society. In the Middle Ages, the penitent's "Book of World Records" was the *Lives* of the desert fathers, famous figures of the fourth and fifth centuries. These *Lives* circulated all over western Europe, translated into Latin and then the vernaculars. In monasteries, they were read at mealtime. In the forests, hermits would recall their stories to each other when they met. The most inspired penitents dreamed of rivaling the exploits of St. Anthony and his fourth-century contemporaries. In late-medieval paintings we see them on their knees, emaciated, in rags, beating their chests with stony blows. Clare doesn't invent anything. She imitates. She commemorates, the way the Mass commemorates the sacrifice of Christ.

She makes the Passion and the sufferings of the martyrs and early Christians present again.

"Lady Clare" had loved good food. But conversion is a complete reversal; so now, "Sister Clare" makes it a point of honor to punish herself in the same way she had sinned. Where once she had dined on savory meat pies, now her "delicate foods" (as the hagiographer puts it, with a certain irony) are a bare minimum of bread and water, adding only a few beans when her companions insist. During the early stages of her conversion, the hagiographer is careful to admit, she would put a little olive oil on her bread for feast days and Sundays. But during Lent, she would give up even bread itself, surviving on just a few raw greens. Her fasts, however, are not determined according to whim, but rather follow the rhythm of the ritual calendar. She carries out Lenten fasts from the feast of St. Martin (November 11) up to Christmas; for forty days after Epiphany (January 6); again for forty days during the "major" Lent leading up to Easter; for two weeks before Pentecost (seven Sundays after Easter) and two weeks before Ascension (forty days after Easter); the evening before feast days of the apostles and that of John the Baptist (June 24); and every Saturday all year long. This schedule adds up to at least 200 fasting days a year, more than most monastic rules of the time prescribed. But it was on par with the other superstars of asceticism, like Radegund before her.

Such a heroic regime, however, could give rise to pride, and hence offered the devil ("the Enemy") an opening for temptation. The *Lives* of the desert fathers are full of similar scenes; the ever-watchful "Enemy of humankind" bides his time, waiting for a moment of weakness. Glorying in her seeming ability "to sustain life without the help of bread and wine," Clare suddenly finds herself beset by satanic temptation. On the verge of giving in, she senses the support of Christ and calls for his aid. If the setup seems the standard stuff of saints' lives, the climax is much less expected. The devil wants her to eat? Fine, she'll eat. But not the delicious foods that the Enemy had expected. Instead, Clare and a female companion find a toad. Clare cuts it up, roasts it, and chokes it down. The disgusting act of chewing and swallowing this "venomous animal" acts like a charm against all future temptation. The devil is defeated by his own tactics. Eating itself has become a penitential act.

Caroline Bynum has masterfully explicated the significance of food and fasting to medieval holy women. The denial of food was not simply modern anorexia—not a "disorder," as we might diagnose it. It was a powerful form of religious expression. Devout medieval women could avoid the normal foods of the family table in favor of those begged as alms. Above all, they turned to the Eucharist, the body of Christ, as spiritual food that nourished a body that, in turn, could suffer like Christ. But Clare adds her own unexpected touch to this picture: the toad. As amphibians who could cross between terrestrial and aquatic worlds, toads and frogs represented the shadowy space between life and death. Thus they frequently appeared along with snakes as elements in the macabre mortuary art of the later Middle Ages, perched next to representations of decomposing corpses. In medieval tales, a liar sometimes ends up spitting toads as a punishment; here, too, this torment is linked with lying. Specifically, the toad was frequently associated with greed, luxury, and female sexuality. Angela of Foligno once confessed, "After I am emptied of this love, I remain so content, so angelic, that I love toads and snakes, and even demons." This is her way of expressing the absolute indifference or annihilation brought on by the presence and absence of divine love. Angela is so far beyond all sense of high and low or good and bad that she even loves toads. Yet even she does not eat them! Clare of Rimini scores a point here not only against the devil but against those other athletes of Christ, her competitors in asceticism.

CHAPTER 4

Far from Home

12. When dissension once again chased her remaining brother out of the city of Rimini, he came to Urbino. There he fell ill for a time, with such a severe illness that doctors feared that he was nearing his end and would die. Hearing this, the servant of God, Sister Clare, moved by a sibling's piety, did not hesitate to go to Urbino, fortified and furnished with everything that she thought would be useful to him, even though it was very painful to her to go far from her homeland.[1] And conferring with the other sisters, she often told them that such a separation for her had been like a preparation for seeing the clear light[2] and the pure truth of her desire. She learned from and was enlightened by the discussions and teachings of many men and women who were full of honesty and right thinking; from them, she attained such an ardor and such a height of penitence that it seemed to her that she did not have time for her ascetic practices, and she feared that she was not chastising herself sufficiently for the transgressions that she had committed and not seeking and finding the cruel torments that she rightly deserved. Nevertheless, she placed her hope in the Lord, thanks to the words of St. Gregory: "The intention of the penitent sinner is fulfilled when the pain of suffering is felt."[3]

13. Having thus settled her brother and provided him with an attendant and a female servant, Sister Clare arranged her daily life in the following manner: there was in the episcopal quarter of Urbino a certain tower, very quiet and worthy of silence, a place most conducive to prayer and spiritual contemplation, as though the very place called out for penitence; here a lamp burned at night, like [a lamp]

that a lady used to keep, as was customary for her to do.[4] In the said episcopal quarter, there was at that time a canon, illuminated by all sanctity, whose life was luminous in its aspect, in speech and good works, as he was known by most prudent men whose lives were true and holy. He was an example and model of right living for all—indeed, a shining mirror of praiseworthy virtue.[5] At night, he continually celebrated in their entirety matins[6] and the other divine offices. Clare confessed to him in secret, and receiving and accepting his honest admonition with goodwill, she prayed that he would allow her to come and attend his offices in the morning. Consenting to her worthy prayers, he ordered that a little entrance be made near the town square, through which she could enter the church at night. And once she had entered, she would sweetly remain there, listening to the word and teaching of God with a great effusion of tears. And right up until nones,[7] she would feel intense delight in her heart because the word of God is more refreshing than any other food. After nones, she would hasten to gather alms door-to-door, not wanting to take or eat her brother's bread. She carried water in a vase from the fountain, and fed herself moderately on bread and water. Somewhat restored and refreshed, if her brother or the serving girl needed something, she would carry it out in all humility.

14. She was in the habit of giving the rest of her bread secretly to the poor who were deprived of all support—hope, faith, and love,[8] with all her effort, converged in her!—so that they would not be forced to steal,[9] or lie, or take the Lord's name in vain[10] through having been reduced by too great a poverty. In sum, the naked were clothed by her efforts.[11] Through her benevolent prayers, prisoners were pardoned[12] and freed from their state by the lords of the lands. She reunited and pacified those who were disrupting the ties of marriage and loving pacts. With her caring hand, she bound the wounds of lepers[13] and felt compassion for all, and comforted them wonderfully, urging patience, saying, "All flesh will soon disappear and decay, because our life is like a bird, in the way it flies quickly through the air to join the sweet nest of its chicks, inclined by natural love."[14] And her sweet and wise speech had such an effect on all those who heard her, that their spirits all inclined to her wishes. And thus she could abundantly give

alms to all the poor and needy. Above all, she sought to be instructed by and to acquire knowledge for salvation from those who were expert in our law and most learned in divine science; and she forced herself to teach those who were ignorant, with great care.

15. It was her habit to confess three, four, or five times a week and, for her more certain salvation, to take communion every Friday. When the sun was setting, actually toward evening, she would make a tour of the churches, returning to the episcopal quarter. And she would stay there until the hour of nones the next day, fervently persevering in prayer in a systematic way, with heartfelt grief, going over her sins with a fine-tooth comb, with groans, tears, and cries, returning again and again in her mind to her old sins of the past, with the words written across from this sign on the fourth page.[15] Since she continued to behave like this, walking barefoot and crying out to God, as explained above, for a long time canons and neighbors, inconvenienced by her constant cries and interrupted in the divine office and in their sleep, not able to correct her of such a practice, told her that she needed to calm herself or quiet down; and if she would not do that, then she would need to leave that place. And so, out of penitence, she agreed to be silent, as long as she could cry out as much as she liked during the day. Leaving the city, almost out of her senses, she returned to gaze upon caves, forests, and valleys. And, above all, she was grieved not to have her own chamber.

16. Once, having returned to Rimini, on the feast of St. Dominic,[16] Sister Clare visited the church of the Preaching Brothers in the morning,[17] with her sister named Druditia.[18] And entering the church, remembering the Passion of our Lord Jesus Christ, the piercing lance,[19] the pressing of the nails, and the other sufferings, she started to shiver, and her teeth began to chatter with an anguished spirit. And in her grief, she fell down and lay as though she were more dead than alive. And the man who was prior of the place at that time, a certain Brother Girolamo, who later was made bishop of the city of Rimini,[20] remembering that she had already told him in confession that such accidents happened to her when she thought of the Lord's Passion, this holy man quickly offered her the consecrated Host. Having received it, she indeed began to recover her health of body and mind. The torment of

such a martyrdom would not have ceased if she had not been helped in such a manner. And from then on, she decided to no longer go to the public and common places where crowds of people flocked.

*   *   *

Clare's family suffered a further blow around 1295. Once the Malatesta family had consolidated its power, Clare's remaining brother was driven out of Rimini. Clare's second husband may have been dead for only a year. She had embraced her religious conversion, but had had only a short time to begin to work out the full implications of her new life of penance. Suddenly, Clare faced a choice between the powerfully competing claims of city and family. To leave for Urbino was to suffer "painful" exile "far from her homeland," even if the two cities are less than sixty kilometers apart. Family loyalty won out. Ultimately, it was a question of duty more than desire: the duty of a medieval woman to care for the men of her family, in sickness and, especially, when death loomed. Moreover, surely another impulse was at work: despite all of Clare's audacity, she needed the protection of the last remaining male member of her family, even in his feeble state.

Strikingly, to this point, Clare's life has been led under the tutelage of one male or another. First her father, then her first husband; and after his death, a return to her father's house. As soon as her father and brother are executed, she remarries. After her second husband's death, and despite her informal religious conversion, she goes to the sickbed of her surviving brother, now the head of the family. Medieval women felt the heavy weight of societal expectations. A woman's reputation depended on maintaining a recognized social status (daughter, wife, nun). Even widowhood did not necessarily imply freedom from the paternal family. Umiliana de' Cerchi, the Florentine holy woman who lived in the first half of the thirteenth century, returned to her father's house following her husband's demise. She refused to remarry, but could not obtain a place in the local Franciscan convent. She turned to penitence, but led her ascetic life within her father's house. Eventually, she became a kind of recluse within a tower that belonged to her family. The symbolism is only too evident: medieval society sought to keep women—especially upper-class women—under firm guard at all stages of life. Paradoxically, a domestic servant, such as the blessed Zita of Lucca (d. 1278), could have considerably more freedom of movement.

These traditional constraints must be understood in order to appreciate fully Clare of Rimini's audacious next steps. She does not abandon her brother but arranges for a domestic servant and a woman to care for him. Even after her conversion, she remains true to a noble lady's domestic responsibilities. But how can she reconcile her family obligations with her newfound dedication to penance? The hagiographer goes to great pains to emphasize that she does not work out the solution alone. Instead, she discusses the question with "many men and women" (the inclusion of women here is far from formulaic) who were "right-thinking." Based on the advice of these unnamed sages of both sexes, Clare reaches new heights of "ardor" for penance, as though she could not possibly endure enough "cruel torments." She crosses the threshold of her brother's home, leaving it behind. The step may have been simpler in Urbino, away from the watchful eyes of family, friends, and neighbors. Clare does not flee to a hermit's solitude in the woods, as a male penitent might have. Like Umiliana de' Cerchi before her, she finds solitude in a tower—but, in this case, it belongs not to her family but to the local cathedral chapter.

The silent, lamp-lit tower seems to call out for solitude, but Clare's move away from her brother requires a new guardian to watch over her spiritual path. An unnamed canon (member of the chapter of clerics that performs the liturgy and work of a cathedral) fills this role, becoming Clare's confessor. Up to five times a week, Clare confesses to him, "in secret," and even obtains permission to have a personal entrance made into his church, so that she can slip in to hear the 3 AM office of matins. In light of this intimate spiritual relationship, with its late-night meetings and secret confessions, no wonder our hagiographer hastens to head off any possible gossip by underlining this man's saintly and virtuous life. But Clare now has her deepest desire: access to the sacred—even if it is through the smallest door (*uscecto*).

Clare is hardly living in strict reclusion. After passing some twelve hours a day (matins to the mid-afternoon office of nones) in tearful prayer, she spends her evenings out in the city, dispensing advice, interceding for the needy, and begging door-to-door for alms to give to the poor. Clare's care for lepers and the poor imitates both Christ and St. Francis. Clare declares her independence by refusing to accept food from her brother, even if she still hastens to his side if he needs anything. Back in her tower, she returns to her past sins in her mind, over and over, crying and groaning. Her neighbors, including the canons, can finally stand it no more—how can they sleep or recite the divine office with all the incessant wailing? After reading the lives of Clare's saintly contemporaries, one is tempted to imagine the walls of Italian cities constantly echoing with the plaintive, penitential cries of an Angela of Foligno or a Margherita of Cortona. At Urbino, Clare's neighbors give her an ultimatum: Quiet down or get out! She agrees to calm down at night; but during the day, she begins to wander into the wild forests and valleys. The ordered space of the city cannot contain the disorder of her spirit.

Clare returned at least once to Rimini during this time, even while her brother still suffered exile. In this sense, a woman might enjoy more freedom than her brothers—political exile was a masculine affair, so Clare could visit her hometown without posing a threat to the Malatesta. On the feast day of St. Dominic (August 5) sometime in the second half of the 1290s, Clare entered the Dominican church with "her sister named Druditia." Although the hagiographer has already mentioned the spiritual "sisters" who would eventually gather around Clare, Druditia seems to be Clare's flesh-and-blood sister. She has not entered the story to this point because the hagiographer has seen fit to focus only on Chiarello's sons. But Druditia's presence at Clare's side increases the historical value of the *Life*. For later events, the spiritual "sisters" who would join Clare could serve as informants to the hagiographer. But how could he have known so many precise details about Clare's early family history? Suddenly, the answer becomes clear: Druditia, who would remain with Clare to the end of her life, is the missing link in this chain of information.

The scene that Druditia must have reported is striking. In the Dominican church, meditating on the suffering of Christ on the cross, Clare begins to shiver, her teeth start to shake, and she collapses to the floor. The Dominican prior Girolamo Fisici brings her around by giving her a consecrated Host, the wafer or body of Christ. Girolamo will be a crucial figure in Clare's later history (see Chapter 12); his importance is foreshadowed by the fact that he is the first named churchman to appear in the text. From his position as Dominican prior of Rimini, Brother Girolamo would rise to be papal penitentiary and chaplain by 1321, and then bishop of Rimini from 1323 until his death in 1328. Reading this account of Clare's swoon and Girolamo's intervention, it is tempting to think of a diabetic on the edge of collapse who needs a quick shot of orange juice to stop from shaking. But Clare's condition is more spiritual than physical. The Host is a sign of the Passion, its very name coming from the Latin *hostia*, meaning "sacrificial victim." For Clare, it is the medicine that relieves the suffering of the Passion, a homeopathic cure in the literal sense of the term.

CHAPTER 5

A Room of One's Own

17. At another time, when peace had been made in Rimini, Sister Clare returned with her brother, servant, and maid; and staying in this same brother's house, since she did not have a place of her own, she would say the entire office according to its order. Then she would visit the churches with a humility that is hard to describe. Finally, she would visit the place of Santa Maria in Muro, to speak in a consoling way with certain worthy and noble ladies from France,[1] who were very famous and outstanding for their widely known good works and virtues. In their garden, or, in other words, the church itself, they would recall the fasts, abstinences, praiseworthy examples, and wise words of various male and female saints, knowing the Gospel passage that says, in the name of God: *Where two or three are gathered in my name, I will be in the midst of them.*[2] This holy company and praiseworthy conversation continued until nones, and she burned with great passion for these activities. Then, as was her custom, abjectly visiting doorways and houses, she would ask for alms; she barely kept herself alive with the bread that she found and the water that she sipped, and she visited peasants and foreigners. With her alms, she supplied miserable people, the needy and the poor, whether they hid this or not, seeing what they needed. To the needy, she carried straw and wood on her own back,[3] always giving thanks to God and to her benefactors, especially in her compensation.

18. Since Sister Clare did not have a room of her own in which she could exercise her devotions, as God, the giver of all graces, watched over her for a long time and gave her in abundance all that she

needed—so that she was an example to all and a mirror of life, especially to Christians and her fellow citizens of Rimini and the surrounding area—inspired by the Divine Spirit, she happily prepared
for herself a little cell in the ancient city walls, with no roof and uncovered, thinking that she had acquired for herself a precious palace
in which she could freely attend to God's word and teachings, which
were so sweet to her. And she made her heart a temple and a little
dwelling-place of Jesus,[4] saying, "Lord, here I can have you!" And she
remembered with loud cries and many tears the entire Passion of
the Cross, and what he had suffered before giving up his spirit, having
compassion for Jesus Christ, who wanted to undergo such tortures for
the sake of us sinners, and similarly for his most sweet mother. And the
more she considered the grave sins she had committed, the more she
wept with many tears in her eyes.

19. But sweet God, who took pleasure in being loved and wanted
to make her heart joyful as she continued in the knowledge of divine
goodness and mercy, raised her heart so high that many times, while
speaking with others, she was rapt and raised up in spirit by the sweetness of the Creator. And she remained suspended, looking at the sky,
as though outside her own perceptions, in such ardor of contemplation
that no matter what was said or done around her, she heard nothing
and knew nothing. And coming back to herself from this elevation
of spirit, as though she had seen the sun or the moon or one of the
stars or a flowering tree, a beautiful bird or a lovely little child, she
rejoiced, filled with desire, thinking of the most gracious works of
God the highest father. And if she knew that God was loved by certain
people, they raised up her spirit in great consolation and joy. Among
other graces she received, she seemed to feel a great warmth in her
heart, and a little child, whole and fully formed, tied to her heart and
moving around.[5] And for this reason, with a lamenting voice, she
called herself an evildoing sinner not worthy of such gifts and graces.

20. At that time, the sisters who were known in Rimini as the
Sisters of Begno were driven out by wars and took refuge in Rimini.[6]
And Sister Clare, having great compassion for them because of the extreme necessity with which they were then afflicted, moved by charity, hurried to visit door-to-door throughout the whole city and in the

suburbs and with her little sack; she made known the miserable poverty of these ladies, alleviating their needs, to their great satisfaction. And since they lacked wood, she found a very heavy stump that she put on her humble back and her head and she carried. Before she could arrive at their place, Sir Dino of the Rossi family,[7] who was her relative, seeing that she was carrying such a stump with great effort, ordered one of his servants to take the stump off the lady's head and have it carried wherever she wanted: "But wish her from me that God may give and offer her always good fortune!" Sister Clare said, "Go away, good man!" He wanted to pay a poor little man to carry it for her, but she did not want to agree to this for anything, as if she had such hate for all the vanities of the world.

21. Her heart had no other desire than to be able to help and to love the poor, and to devote all her care to consoling the troubled. It happened that a person afflicted with many troubles needed to send someone to Urbino, in a time of great snow and ice and cold. And so Sister Clare, with a happy and joyful countenance, set off on the road and quickly performed this service and returned. Those who saw her in such a fury of winds and air said to her, "O hopeless woman, you are going to meet your death! What necessity pushes you to die?" And her feet were still spilling an abundant amount of blood, due to the cold. Sister Clare did everything conquered by charity, and by zeal for consoling the afflicted and the suffering. At night, she would sleep in a wet and frozen tunic, and she would not change it getting into or out of bed, if there was a bed for her to rest in. Nor did these tribulations cause her any illness because the interior heat overcame the exterior [cold], and she did everything intending to please God in all things and through all things, since God asks nothing more than his entire creature.[8]

22. Sister Clare was in the habit of closely examining her conscience in the evening, and she took it into her head to correct what was not proper, and to carry out and practice good, worthy, and holy things. She gloried in the Lord for works well done[9] and bemoaned those that were done badly. In the morning, confessing to the priest, she would ask for correction and pardon, and she would take on even more penances than the priest imposed on her, considering how she

had failed such a humble Lord, while she had received and was receiving day and night such excellent gifts from him. Then she would beat
herself cruelly with an iron chain, and, battered with this martyrdom,
she would beat her chest with a stone, beyond measure. She would not
cease such a charge until she was overcome by pain and fatigue, and
she would lie down as though she were half dead. And if she fell back
into the same sin, she would double her self-punishment.

23. Since she visited houses every day to seek alms, when she was
asked if she was gathering them for herself, she answered yes. After
saying that, her conscience began to bother her, saying, "You crazy
woman, do you want to lose your soul by lying?" And she wanted to
confess this to the priest, who responded: "Since you did this for the
sake of charity, I absolve you and I free you of this sin." One time, she
received alms from the house of a certain person, on the vigil of Pentecost, in order to help a poor and ashamed family; when she was
asked if she had been at the house of a certain lady, she answered no.
And thus, as you will hear, she wanted to chastise herself for such a
lie, so that, finding the said lady in the church, she said, "My lady,
when you asked me if I had come from the house of that lady, I said
no, and in doing so I was lying to you." The lady answered, "I don't
remember you." "Certainly, you recognize me!" said Sister Clare, "and
it was a lie when I denied it to you. For the love of God, I beg your
pardon."

24. Another time, when it happened that she had said a word that
was not quite proper, right away she shut herself in the cell, pulled out
her tongue, clasped it with pincers, and left it bound up like that for
almost an entire week. And believing that she had done the necessary
penance for this sin, she wanted to free her tongue; but she could
not, because it was too swollen, there having flowed a great deal of
blood because of the pain. She remained silent like this for many
days, unable to talk. In this way, she was cured of this vice and others.
Demand and ask that with the help of God, the soul may achieve mas-
tery and lordship over the flesh as it ought![10]

25. And from then on, she received a most curbed tongue, most
gracious to listeners and most pleasant to everyone, and most filled
with seriousness of judgment in offering the highest things of God,

so as to accomplish the Gospel, which says: *It is no longer you who speaks, but it is the Spirit of God that speaks in you.*[11] In this way, people, both foreigners and peasants, rushing to her with solicitude, listened to her castigating pronouncements. Anyone who was troubled was consoled by this. Similarly, evil and dishonest people, hearing her wise words, seemed to rejoice and find peace in their souls, so much so that for her listeners, a long time would seem short, as she admonished many people and called many to her.

26. Now, to conclude briefly concerning her speech, married women and unmarried and other ladies removed their necklaces and jewelry; lascivious women became honest and eager for chastity; all of them learned about the charity of God. She led countless clerics and laypeople to penitence.

* * *

When civic peace at last returned to Rimini, Clare and her brother could regain their native city. The date is not certain, but it must have been fairly close to 1300, when Clare was about forty years old and the Malatesta clan were firmly installed as rulers of the city. At first, Clare stayed at her brother's home. What else could she do, since "she did not have a place of her own"? There she adopted a quasi-monastic routine, passing her days by reciting the divine office, or canonical hours (matins about 3 AM; lauds at dawn; prime about 6 AM; terce about 9 AM; sext about noon; nones about 3 PM; vespers about 6 PM; compline before retiring to bed). But Clare was driven to break her remaining familial bonds by her desire to have a place for herself. The hagiographer stresses this idea repeatedly. Clare had experienced a taste of autonomy in her tower at Urbino. The return to Rimini paradoxically threatened to re-impose limits on her movements and meditations. With no way to carve out this space in her brother's home, Clare strikes out on her own.

The impulse to possess a private, personal space for reflection is hardly a modern innovation. Clare voices the same cry that Virginia Woolf would express six centuries later: "A room of one's own!" Of course, it would be unhelpful to imagine her as a proto-feminist in the modern sense. Yet it is not entirely anachronistic to see Clare's move as an insistence on her own autonomy. For under whose authority does she now live? Not her father's or husband's or

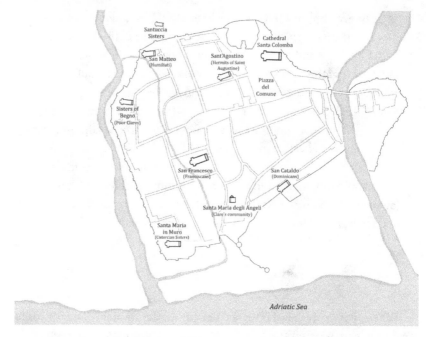

Map 2. Religious communities of Rimini, as shown on the earliest surviving map of Rimini (1617). © M. Cecilia Gaposchkin. Based on an engraving by Alfonso Arrigoni in Cesare Clementini, *Raccolto istorico della fondatione di Rimino e dell'origine, e vite de' Malatesti* (Rimini, 1617), vol. 2 (end of volume, no p. no.). Note that Clare's community is here identified by its later name of Santa Maria degli Angeli and that a long process of silting left the city walls farther from the harbor in 1617 than they would have been in Clare's lifetime.

brother's. Only God's. It was God (says our hagiographer) who inspired Clare to settle in a little cell in the remnants of the old Roman walls of Rimini, fallen into disuse after more ample fortifications were constructed in the thirteenth century. Clare's sense of triumph suffuses her cry, "Lord, here I can have you!" The move to her cell is not a retreat but a conquest, a victory that opens up new possibilities. With her hard-won freedom, Clare now begins to construct a kind of female network in the city, developing her own ties to nuns, secular ladies, and poor women.

Our hagiographer has already alluded to Clare's cell in Chapter 3, but now provides detail. Her little enclosure is literally a hole-in-the-wall. Lacking a roof, it encloses without offering any real protection. Clare has succeeded in appropriating ("she prepared for herself") a room to call her own but hardly a place to find rest. At night, awake and cold in the rain, she examines her conscience instead of sleeping, meditating on her own sins and on Jesus's suffering on the cross. She glories in thoughts of her good works, but then confesses this pride in the morning. Well beyond the priest's assigned penance, she punishes her body with heavy blows. Moreover, a room of her own does not preclude a willingness to travel in aid of others. When an unnamed person "afflicted with many troubles" needs someone to run an errand to Urbino, Clare sets off through the snow and ice, back to the city where she had once shared her brother's exile. By the time she returns from her journey, her feet are bloody with frostbite.

For Clare, personal space does not produce personal peace. The fear of lying torments her. Our hagiographer recounts a seemingly banal story about how, after having falsely claimed that the alms that she gathered were for herself, Clare repents and rushes to confess her sin. The priest assures her that in protecting the identity of those who need charitable aid, she is acting in good faith. Still, she obsesses over having said something untrue. Then, in what seems an almost comically convoluted scene, Clare tries to tell one "lady" that she had lied when denying having been at the house of another "lady," but the first lady claims to have no idea what she's talking about! Clare nevertheless begs for forgiveness. Saying the wrong thing is Clare's constant fear. So she adopts a hideously literal remedy, clasping her tongue in pincers to avoid any further sins of speech. The scene in which she then cannot get her swollen tongue free might again seem almost comical, were it not so brutally bloody.

Speech and food, the tongue and the mouth: again and again, Clare's sins and triumphs return to these themes. In her youthful married life, it had been her eating and drinking that obsessed her. Now she feeds the poor, and penitent words punctuate her conversion, yet she is never free of the fear of speaking falsely. Clare's contemporary the German Premonstratensian canoness Christina of Hane (c. 1269–c. 1292) was said to have bitten her tongue until it bled in order to keep from saying an angry word. Italian holy women, those who had known the world's pleasures and repented of them, also linked food and fast with falsity and truth. The most famous and startling example is provided by Angela of Foligno. Once, at Lent, Angela dreamed of going naked through town with fish and meats draped around her neck, crying, "Here is the most vile of women, full of malice and deceit, the path of all vice and evil, who pretended to fast in her cell. . . . In reality, I was a glutton, full of appetite, greedy and drunk. . . . I want to have a halter put on my neck and be dragged through the cities and squares so that the children will lead me around and say, 'Here is the woman who presented false for true her whole life!'" Like Clare, Angela blends her worries about speaking the truth with her fears and fantasies around food.

If Clare has found a new home in the city walls, she has certainly not walled herself off from her city. Clare makes the rounds of the city's churches, including Santa Maria in Muro and the Sisters of Begno. Santa Maria "at the Wall" (*in Muro*) was located near Clare's cell, where the ancient city wall met the ruins of the old Roman amphitheater (see Map 2). Since 1265, Santa Maria in Muro had sheltered Cistercian nuns who had fled from Constantinople. From 1204 (when French crusaders and Venetian sailors had stormed Constantinople) to 1265 (when the Greeks had at last pushed out the "Latin" interlopers), imperial Constantinople had been dominated by French-speaking nobles—hence the surprising reference by our hagiographer to "worthy and noble ladies from France" who had taken refuge in Rimini. Clare does not seem to have been in the least bit intimidated by these "very famous" nuns. Together, every morning, they gather and discuss the words and deeds of saintly men and women. But in the afternoon, inflamed by the spiritual ardor kindled by these conversations, Clare goes out into the city, begging for food to give to the needy and the poor. For the moment, she does not seek to be a model for anyone; rather, she wants to work on behalf of others, to share her bread, her words, and her knowledge.

The Sisters of Begno were nuns of the Order of St. Clare. Like the Cistercians of Santa Maria in Muro, they were refugees in Rimini. In 1288, local wars had forced them out of their original home at Castello di Begno (or Castelbegni) near San Leo, some thirty kilometers (nineteen miles) southwest of Rimini. Clare of Assisi (d. 1253) had been St. Francis's most ardent adherent, crafting a life of enclosed poverty for her community of San Damiano, just outside Assisi. The papally sponsored rule for the Order of St. Clare, ratified in 1263, severely watered down the life of poverty for which Clare of Assisi had fought, instead offering a firmly enclosed existence for nuns within the orbit of the Franciscan family. But during their difficult years as refugees in Rimini (until 1306), the Sisters of Begno were indeed poor, afflicted by "extreme necessity." And so—irony of ironies—it is Clare of Rimini whose freedom of movement allows her to provide for the "Clarissan" nuns by begging door-to-door, just as Francis had done. But the Franciscan nuns lacked not only food but wood, so Clare struggles to bring them a heavy stump. It is here that the hagiographer introduces Clare's "relative," Sir Dino of the Rossi family. Seeing Clare struggle along with this burden, he tries to have a servant carry it for her, but she will have none of it.

Clare now begins to assume the role of teacher, imparting her words of wisdom to others. In theory, the right to offer the word of God belonged only to male clerics. Visionary women, such as the learned twelfth-century abbess Hildegard of Bingen, might overcome this prohibition by claiming that it was not they who spoke, but God who spoke through them. Clare takes a more literal and visceral route to justifying her authority. First (in Chapter 4), she "learned from" the teachings of wise men and women; but quickly, her "sweet and wise speech" began to affect others, and she "forced herself to teach those who were ignorant." Now, in her own room, she has quite literally disciplined her tongue, keeping it bound up for a week until "she received a most curbed tongue, most gracious to listeners." It is this hard-won transformation, according to our hagiographer, that lends Clare "seriousness of judgment in offering the highest things of God," so that (in the words of Matt. 10:20) it is now the spirit of God that speaks in her. Now she distributes not only alms but words and knowledge. Now "foreigners and peasants" flock to her to hear her admonitions; "evil and dishonest people" find peace in her pronouncements; her "speech" causes women to discard their vain jewelry and embrace chastity; and even "countless clerics" are led to penitence by her words. A room of one's own is a powerful thing.

CHAPTER 6

The Shadow of Heresy

27. A certain highly educated friar, at a certain moment, cast off the habit of the Order and strayed seriously from the path of the light of truth. By the action of God, he went to Sister Clare, and as they spoke together, she said to him, "What do you think, friar or good man (*bono homo*)?" And he answered, "I want to be a soldier." After humbly admonishing him, she left him in peace. And when he had left her, she actually knelt and she prayed to God, day and night, with great tears and suffering, that this wayward man would return to the clarity of the light of truth. Two days later, he returned to her and said, "I want to obey you and do what you advise me." So Sister Clare had him eat, and she dressed him in a religious habit, and placed him in a certain other monastery—since he did not want to return to his own—where he lived and died, leading an excellent life. Since the neighborhood where Sister Clare stayed was filled with evil people who committed adultery and murder there, thanks to her it was reformed and made suitable and honest.

28. *God corrects and chastises* who *loves* Him.[1] So that her intrinsic perfection would be evident,[2] God allowed certain preachers to say from the pulpit that she was a patarine,[3] and out of order, and that she had an unclean spirit in her. Then they railed with furious words: "Lords and ladies and all you others, watch out for that woman! She is certainly the demon who attacks you under the false guise of humility, because she howls like a wolf, hisses like a serpent, and moos like a cow. And only one person like her is found in all of scripture, and that was the Canaanite woman who sought out Jesus and asked

him to free her daughter from an unclean spirit;[4] and she howled, too. I tell you that this woman is a perfidious patarine! Be sure that your wives do not keep any company with her!" And thus she was shunned by all the women. But the spirit of God taught her and guided her and reassured her, so that she attended all the sermons, bravely present, as though nothing bad was being said about her. And the one who was preaching abandoned his topic in order to preach about her, pointing his finger at her: "Flee this wretched little sister (*sorecta*) because the evil spirit controls her and rules her!" And at the end of the sermon, children chased after her, mocking her and saying, "It's the patarine!" And they hurled stones at her. But when she was back in her cell, her mind was pleasantly peaceful and happy. And she told her sisters more than once that this episode was the greatest consolation that she ever received in her life. These rumors about her went on for a year. During this time, when she heard the friar preaching in the pulpit and saying what was described above, she would *glory in the Lord*[5] and say, "These words have been the most useful and consoling to me that I have ever received." When it pleased God, however, these rumors ceased.

29. A great usurer of Rimini, named Amadio, slandering her, mocked her greatly. And she was confirmed by God with greater grace. In the meantime, her good reputation grew so that everyone, both far and near, considered themselves to have received a special grace not from speaking with her but just by seeing her. And not only laypeople but very well-educated men were pleased with the gracefulness of her words, and they marveled at her wisdom and her holy life, saying, "This woman is truly the servant of God."[6] When certain catholic and spiritual people came to her from a far-off village, alone at that time and with no other female companion, she led them, like religious and honest people, to certain good houses. And right away, she supplied them with food to eat according to their rank because, going to the town square, she obtained what she asked for, on credit from the shopkeepers. And she brought these things to the houses of certain religious people, seeing to it that they were cooked and carried. And so that the people she had left there could be sure to eat, she brought an abundance of what they desired, in a certain basket.

Then, by asking and begging alms in the houses, she paid what was owed, because her words were of such grace that almost no one could refuse what she asked. And often, thinking about it, she would say, "It saddens my spirit that I cannot supply all the people I visit with what they need; and it makes me even sadder that I have no place to live."

*   *   *

Just three little paragraphs make up Chapter 6, but they are rich in significance. The chapter seems to begin innocently. A "certain highly educated friar" approaches Clare. This brother, probably a Franciscan, has fled his order. Clare's question to him is blunt: Do you want to remain a friar or become a good man (*bono homo* in Italian)? The opposition might seem odd; does Clare mean to say that friars (members of the mendicant orders) are not good men? The most likely reading is that Clare framed the man's choice as between being a humble friar (*frate*) or a respectable member of lay society (*bono homo*). But a less obvious reading is worth considering. In medieval usage, *bono homo* could sometimes indicate a leader within groups labeled as heretical by the church. Modern historians have long tended to lump these heretics together under the name "Cathars"; but within their own circles, they were more often called "good men," "good women," or "good Christians." The *Life* of Clare alternates between chronological and thematic chapters. The theme of Chapter 6, as we shall see, is the way suspicion of heresy falls onto Clare. Thus our hagiographer may have wanted to begin the chapter by having Clare counsel a man she believes to be fleeing his order to join a group of religious dissidents. In any case, the educated friar quickly clears himself of this suspicion—he just wants to be a soldier! Probably, Clare is relieved. After all, Francis of Assisi once dreamed of martial glory himself. So she leaves the friar alone and allows him time to think. When he returns, she offers him, instead of a lecture, something to eat. What man would have thought of this reassuring method of refreshing a wayward soul? Thanks to Clare, he finds a renewed place in the world by adopting the habit of another order. Yet, as is so often the case in this *Life*, Clare oversteps the bounds of a simple laywoman's position; for a friar to move from his order to another "monastery" under another rule should have required ecclesiastical sanction. For Clare to "place" him there on her own authority was audacious, indeed.

If heresy has now reared its head, the reader may suddenly wonder what danger Clare herself has been running. Indeed, we now learn that her unregulated life of penance has raised the suspicions of some members of the local clergy, and Clare begins to suffer attacks from the pulpit, as preachers in Rimini thunder against her. What are her offenses, in the eyes of these accusers? She is a "patarine" (*paterina*) with an "unclean spirit in her"; she is a "demon" feigning humility in order to deceive; she howls and hisses and moos; she threatens to lead respectable women astray; she is ruled by an "evil spirit." For a full year, sometime between 1300 and 1306, she is singled out, mocked, and shunned.

The hagiographer marvels at her daring, but we might just as well marvel at his. He was, after all, composing a saint's life, a text that was supposed to edify and praise. For a saint to be tempted by the devil or reviled by the impenitent is expected; but for churchmen to turn against the penitent, and for her hagiographer to stress that fact, is highly unusual. Sometimes, reading between the lines of hagiographic texts, scholars pick up hints of tensions between a charismatic saint and the institutional church. But to explicitly devote a chapter of a hagiographic legend to the hero's direct conflict with ecclesiastical authorities passes all usual limits of the genre.

Of what is Clare accused? The word that sums up the allegations, bellowed by the preacher and echoed by jeering children, is "patarine." The term originally referred to an eleventh-century group in Milan known for attacking the corruption of local clerics. The papacy at the time of the Gregorian Reform actually protected this group and supported its ends, hoping to channel the patarines' energy into its own reform movement. But once the church hierarchy had achieved most of its reforming goals, troublemaking laypeople like these Milanese activists were viewed with a less tolerant eye. Thus, by the twelfth century, "patarine" had taken on an entirely negative meaning and become a generic way of referring to someone accused of heresy, particularly someone who stubbornly challenged ecclesiastical authority. The label was certainly used in this way in thirteenth-century Rimini. In fact, a much later source (Monsignor Giacomo Villani, a local scholar writing in the seventeenth century) reports that in the 1250s, "all the houses and buildings of the patarines were sacked and destroyed . . . and the whole neighborhood, that is the area that they inhabited at Rimini . . . was eternally held in anathema up to the present, reduced largely to fields and gardens, from the mill named after these patarines, near the cloister *degli Angeli*, to the nuns of the Abbesses, in the place now known as San Martino." This neighborhood is exactly the part of Rimini in which Clare established her cell (Santa Maria degli Angeli would be the successor community to her followers). Her place of dwelling, in an area already infamous for its heretical reputation, may have helped attract the negative label of "patarine." Even our heroine's *Life* reckons that "the neighborhood where Sister Clare stayed was filled with evil people who committed adultery and murder."

Who were Clare's unnamed antagonists? The label "preachers" might seem to suggest members of the Dominican Order, known as the "Preaching Brothers." Moreover, this possibility might seem intrinsically likely, given Dominicans' affinity for the office of inquisitor. Since the 1230s, popes had designated individual friars as "inquisitors of heretical depravity," and in much of western Europe, it was Dominicans who assumed this role. In Rimini, however, it is more likely that the attacks against Clare would have emanated from the hagiographer's own order. In 1254, Pope Innocent IV had placed Franciscans in charge of inquisitions in the region of Romagna; in 1259, Alexander IV divided their jurisdiction so that one Franciscan inquisitor would sit in Faenza and a second in Rimini. If a friar in Rimini was attacking Clare as part of an official charge to root out heresy, he would have been a figure such as Tommasino Malebranchi of Parma, the Franciscan inquisitor active in Rimini between 1298 and 1305, or his vicar Vincenzo of Bologna. Indeed, if the attacks on Clare were not merely denunciations but inquisitorial accusations of heresy, the first step could have been excommunication for a year, the length of time our author indicates that Clare suffered these indignities.

Whether or not an inquisitor launched a formal accusation of heresy against her, Clare was certainly singled out, publicly, from the pulpits of Rimini by several preachers in the course of their duties. She was considered guilty of heresy—if not in an inquisitorial court, then at least in the court of public opinion—and she was shunned by polite society. For these hostile preachers, Clare has only the "false guise of humility." Saints were truly humble, whereas heretics were known to feign this quality in order to mislead the credulous and unwary. Even worse: Clare is inhabited by an "unclean spirit" (*spirito inmundo*) or demon; indeed, the text insists that "she *is* certainly the demon" herself. What is the proof? Her bestial noises. "She howls like a wolf, hisses like a serpent, and moos like a cow." When Clare had wailed at night in Urbino, it had been perceived as a nuisance. But this behavior is now said to reveal her bestial impulses, her commerce with the Beast.

But after hurling the term "patarine" (with its generic connotations of stubborn heresy) and launching allegations of behavior befitting the possessed, the preacher makes an unexpected comparison. In all of scripture, he says, only one person like Clare can be found: the Canaanite woman. The Gospel of Matthew (15:21–23) relates her story:

> And Jesus went from there, and retired into the coasts of Tyre and Sidon. And behold, a Canaanite woman came out of those coasts, crying out, and said to him, "Have mercy on me, O Lord, son of David: my daughter is grievously troubled by a demon." He answered her not a word. And his disciples came and besought him, saying, "Send her away, for she cries after us." And he, answering, said, "I was sent only to the sheep who are lost of the house of Israel." But she came and adored him, saying, "Lord, help me." He, answering, said, "It is not good to take the bread of the children, and to cast it to the dogs." But she said, "Yea, Lord; for the whelps also eat of the crumbs that fall from the table of their masters." Then Jesus, answering, said to her, "O woman, great is thy faith. Let it be done to you as you wish." And her daughter was cured from that hour.

The same raw elements are indeed present in the *Life of Clare* as in the Gospel of Matthew: a woman, demonic possession, infuriating howls. But the preacher of Rimini twists the meaning of the Gospel story. Although the Canaanite's cries annoy Christ's disciples, it is not she who is possessed, but her daughter. More important, the faith of the mother (the Canaanite herself) is ultimately praised and rewarded after her exquisite rejoinder to Jesus's initial reluctance. The preacher of Rimini—perhaps carried away with "furious words" at the very thought of Clare wailing, wandering the streets, and usurping churchmen's right to teach—evokes a biblical passage involving a woman and demonic possession. But in his rage, he points to a female figure who stands for the very opposite of his intended meaning. Our Franciscan hagiographer records Clare's clash with authority, but at the same time slyly mocks his brother's muddled comparison.

To whom was the preacher really speaking? At first, he claims to address everyone: "Lords and ladies and all you others." But by the end of his first tirade, he is speaking only to the husbands, assumed to have power over their wives: "Be sure that your wives do not keep any company with her!" This is what is really at stake: the power of a female network that threatens to circumvent men's institutional power. And so for the preacher, it is the demon that has driven Clare to speak with her spiritual friends—the Cistercians of Santa Maria in Muro, the Poor Clares of Begno—and to beg from charitable well-off women to aid the less fortunate. She should be silenced, chastised, and restrained.

Our hagiographer ends the chapter by turning the tables on Clare's tormenters. If she has been mocked by little children, now it is a "great usurer of Rimini, named Amadio" who slanders her. The man's name means "love God" (*ama Dio*); the hagiographer probably enjoys underlining this irony as an indication of the way religious faith in Rimini has been perverted by greed. "Usurer" is one of the nastiest insults that can be hurled at someone in this society, with popes and emperors alike fulminating against rapacious moneylenders in Rimini and elsewhere. To be insulted by a notorious usurer is thus almost a compliment. Clare and her rejection of riches stand in opposition to this reviled figure. Specifically, when detailed records of inquisitorial activity in the Romagna emerge during 1320–1340 (just as our hagiographer was writing), usury turns out to be the most frequent cause of condemnation. Thus the roles are reversed, and Clare functions as an ally of the inquisitors. The *Life* can now abruptly assert that Clare's "good reputations grew," and people—even the highly educated, like the friar whose dilemma opened the chapter—come from far and wide to see "the servant of God."

Our hagiographer is deceptively sophisticated; heresy is introduced as a potentially scandalous issue in the chapter's central episode but carefully folded between opening and closing anecdotes that show Clare herself as a champion of orthodoxy. The *Life* faithfully records the accusations of heresy but softens the blow, absorbs the shock, and turns defeat into triumph by making a sign of infamy into proof of election in the eyes of God. Clare has suffered like Christ, been reviled in his name. Now she can return to

her accustomed activities of finding food for the hungry—this time, not by
simply begging but by obtaining credit from willing shopkeepers. Their gen-
erosity stands as an implicit rebuke to Amadio the usurer, and Clare pays
back what she owes after she is able to beg door-to-door.

*   *   *

It is impossible to understand the European Middle Ages without facing the
question of heresy. It is against heresy, and therefore through heresy, that
Christianity and the church are defined, the way a wall excluding the exterior world defines the city within. For a long time, historians thought of
medieval heresies as organized sects—anti-churches, each with its own hierarchy, doctrines, and rites. Scholars speculated on their exotic eastern
origins—all real heresies were supposed to come from the "Orient," which is
to say, from the eastern "Other." In this view, heresies like the "Cathars" had
underground existences with secret initiations that helped them to survive,
undetected, for centuries, from the days of Augustine to the era of the inquisitors, eternal and unchanging. At its best, this kind of scholarship could
draw erudite genealogies for specific ideas; at its worst, it could encourage
the kind of conspiratorial thinking that would have the Templars as the first
European settlers of New England. More seriously, this approach risked mis-
taking what medieval churchmen say about heresy as sure evidence for heresy itself. In fact, theologians' tracts and inquisitors' manuals reveal more
about what churchmen thought than what "heretics" believed. From the 1950s
through the 1970s, another materialist approach to history, more or less Marx-
ist, saw heresy as a reflection of social tensions or as a manifestation of out-
right class warfare. This school of thought tried to apply social theory to
structures of religious dissidence but ultimately did not succeed—too many
nobles and wealthy townspeople embraced the "wrong" side of this supposed
war. Religious deviance and disbelief did exist in the Middle Ages, but attempts to organize it into settled sects or social classes have remained
problematic.

Clare's case is instructive. By now, we know, in broad strokes, what there
is to know about her life. She does not belong to a secret sect. She obeys no
heresiarch from the East. She does not pass her nights in torch-lit caves practicing diabolical rites. Instead, she is obsessed by the Passion, besotted with

Christ. She tries fervently to put the precepts of the Gospels into practice as literally as possible: to help the poor, to spread the word of God, and to imitate the teachings of the saints. But she takes things to extremes. She cries too loudly, claims too much independence, offends too many sensibilities, teaches too boldly, acts on her own authority (for instance, in transferring a friar to another monastery). Thus, outraged preachers single her out from the pulpit, with all their official authority, and level their charges: she is a patarine, a heretic; she is a demon, a devil, a danger. In this very moment, heresy is brought to life, made flesh and blood in Clare. It is the preacher who makes Clare a heretic.

How does she react? She rejoices—at least, according to our hagiographer. Back in her cell, she feels peace. For did not the Lord say, "Blessed are you when they shall revile you and persecute you and speak all that is evil against you, untruly, for my sake. Be glad and rejoice, for your reward is very great in heaven!" (Matt. 5:11–12). Thus fortified, Clare refuses to keep a low profile. To the contrary, she shows up for every sermon, "bravely" facing her accusers. Her brazen certainty in the Lord infuriates the preacher; his redoubled accusations make her more convinced than ever that she is on the path of righteousness. Both sides need each other to reinforce their certainties. This little episode is like a laboratory experiment demonstrating the invention of heresy.

"God corrects and chastises who loves him." This is how our hagiographer opens his account of Clare's brush with heresy. The Italian quotation clearly comes from the book of Proverbs; but there, it is God who "chastises whom he loves." The shift is slight, but the formulation in the *Life* grants more importance to the human who draws God's correction by means of his or her love. Such slips in biblical quotations can be revealing. Recall the opening of Chapter 3, where Clare cries out, "Do penance, and the kingdom of heaven will arrive in you!" (*Fate penitentia et se aproximarà in voi el regno de' celi!*). Clearly, Clare echoes the book of Matthew, where John the Baptist first announces: "Do penance, for the kingdom of heaven is at hand!" (*Poenitentiam agite, appropinquavit enim regnum caelorum!* [3:2]), and the same words are then spoken by Jesus (4:17).

The difference between the canonical text of the Vulgate (the Latin Bible) and what we find in the Italian *Life* of Clare might seem minor; but in this case, it could matter a great deal. The biblical phrase in its original context is a warning: Repent now, for the End is near. But this is not what Clare's phrasing implies. As our hagiographer reports it, this wording suggests that if one does penance, the kingdom of heaven will arrive, not just in time (chronologically) but "in you." Personal penitence is thus a means to perfection, in the here and now, without the mediation of priests or the church. The link between the two slightly shifted biblical phrases (God corrects and chastises who loves him; do penance, and the kingdom of heaven will arrive in you) is an insistence on humans' active role in achieving salvation—an insistence that could be interpreted by a hostile audience as doctrinal deviance. Although Clare would almost certainly not have known the word, a learned churchman might have called this "Pelagianism," the heresy (named after the fifth-century theologian Pelagius) of insisting that humans can simply use free will to choose good over evil, thanks to human effort, not God's grace.

In fact, it was nothing of the kind, but merely the result of the way Clare (as recorded by her hagiographer) had patched together several Latin biblical passages and rendered them too literally into Italian. Very similar passages in the book of Luke (17:21) say, "Behold, the kingdom of God is within you (*intra vos est*)," and "the kingdom of God is drawn near to you (*appropinquavit in vos*)" (10:9). For learned churchmen, the fine distinctions between each of these formulations could be maintained; for a layperson soaking up what she heard from the pulpit, all these statements about the kingdom of God/heaven must have melted into one another. The problem is that in Latin, the preposition *in* plus a noun in the accusative case (*vos*) indicates "motion toward" ("to you"). But if the same phrasing is copied slavishly into Italian (*in voi*), it means "in you." The tense of the verb in Clare's phrasing is similarly explained by recourse to biblical texts. The Vulgate reading in Matthew and Luke is *appropinquavit*, which is in the perfect tense and expresses action in the past. But Clare lived before the invention of the printing press. Every copy of the Bible (and every other book) was written by hand, and each one was a little different from every other. Scribes introduced variations, either by accident or on purpose, and some of these variant readings had long lives. In this case, a long manuscript tradition stood behind reading the passage in question as *appropinquabit*. The change from a *v* to a *b* puts the Latin verb in the future tense. Thus Clare's Italian (*se aproximarà*) simply follows this variant version of the Vulgate. Some of the greatest schoolmen of the thirteenth century, including Thomas Aquinas, had wrestled with the same reading, seeking to explain how it should properly be understood.

But if Clare intended no doctrinal deviance, that does not mean that she ran no risks. In 1260, as the Franciscan chronicler Salimbene tells us, Gherardo Segarelli, founder of the sect known as the pseudo-apostles, walked the streets of Parma, crying, *Penitençagite*, because he did not know how to say *Poenitentiam agite* ("do penance"). His followers were accused of heresy for adopting a too radical stance on absolute poverty and criticizing the church for its lax ways. After Gherardo was burned at the stake in 1300, the even more radical Fra Dolcino took leadership over the pseudo-apostles. In his *Practice of the Inquisition*, written about the same time as the *Life of Clare*, the Dominican Bernard Gui explained how to root out the members of Dolcino's sect; their rallying cry was the very verse of the book of Matthew that we have been examining, expressed in the future tense. Indeed, other records confirm that the apostles called out this verse, in the future tense, in the streets of Bologna, like a chant.

Clare is not a learned theologian. She mulls over biblical phrases that she has heard, repeating them in her mind and molding them to her own vernacular language. But as the apostle Paul says, "the letter kills." A few little letters, a *b* for a *v*, led Gherardo Segarelli to the stake in 1300 and, after him, Dolcino and his companion Margherita in 1307. If our Franciscan hagiographer dares to quote Clare in her exact words, it may be because he thinks it possible to slip in this ambiguous utterance once he has sufficiently underlined the radical orthodoxy of Clare's approach to penance. Still, he puts dangerous words in his heroine's mouth.

*   *   *

Clare's case also stands at the culmination of a long buildup of anti-heretical machinery in Rimini. As early as 1185, Pope Lucius III had written to the bishop of Rimini, claiming that the "leaders of the patarines" had returned to the city. These heretics were accused of refusing to pay tithes and practicing usury, and the pope threatened interdict (suspending all church services and sacraments) if the city fathers did not swear an oath to expel heresy. Similar injunctions were repeated for Rimini by Emperor Henry VI in 1196 and Pope Innocent III in 1204. In 1226, the *podestà* tried to have certain women

of the city burned as heretics, but was attacked and thwarted by their relatives. About the same time, the Franciscan Anthony of Padua came to preach
in Rimini because it was reputed to be infested with heresy. Convinced by
his sermon, a leading heretic called Bononillus or Bonivillus renounced his
errors—very likely, this was Arimino of Bonfiletto, a ringleader of the attack
on the *podestà*. Nothing in this early period suggests real doctrinal deviancy
among these "heretics." Nor were the attempts to suppress their flouting of
church authority (indifference to tithes and strictures against usury) well organized or effective.

That would have begun to change by the 1250s, with the arrival of Franciscan inquisitors in Rimini. Sometime after 1261 (just about the time of
Clare's birth), a woman named Mirabella was charged by the inquisitors as a
leader of patarines in Rimini and nearby Faenza. A surviving deposition from
Alberigo of the Manfredi family, whom Dante would call "the vilest spirit of
Romagna" (*Inferno* XXXIII, 154), accuses her of teaching how patarines were
to be greeted, by saying, "Bless you, good Christians," and that she "preached"
heresy; specifically, that the body of Christ consecrated by priests was worth-
less, as were priests and bishops themselves. Alberigo even provided a list of
twenty-four names of those who "believed" in Mirabella. If the accusations
are true, here is a case involving actual doctrinal deviance. At the same time,
the inquisitors did not have smooth sailing. Three times in the early 1270s they
had to threaten the council of the Rimini Commune with excommunication
for anyone who impeded their inquisitions. A lay official working for the
inquisitors was even assassinated.

But the period in which the Malatesta took the city firmly in hand was
also the moment in which inquisitorial power solidified. In 1299–1300, forty
citizens were appointed to form a lay tribunal to support the Franciscan inquisitors. Around the same time, inquisitorial documents from Rimini were
used to create compilations for the use of inquisitors. The combination of lay
and inquisitorial powers is nicely exemplified by the fact that the notary
Zanchino Ugolini helped create the lay tribunal in 1299–1300, wrote the
Treatise on the Material of Heretics around 1330, and played a key role in the
revision of Rimini's communal statutes in 1334. The Commune, which had
long been hostile to the bishop, was now reshaped by the Malatesta clan to
become the zealous ally of the inquisitors. The very clan that had exiled and

executed Clare's family members now brought inquisitorial power within its orbit as well.

It was exactly at this moment that "certain preachers," who may have been Franciscan inquisitors, let loose against Clare. They call her a "patarine," just as they did Mirabella a generation earlier. But Clare does not share Mirabella's doubts about the Eucharist. Instead, the clerical accusations here introduce a new element: demonic possession. During the twelfth century and through the first three-quarters of the thirteenth, bishops and inquisitors had worried little about divinations and demons. Early inquisitors sought to break up networks of supposed heretics; they were not interested in "superstitions" and what they regarded as the fantasies of old women. But the decades on either side of 1300 saw what Alain Boureau has called a "demonological turning point." By 1326, Pope John XXII would link sorcery to heresy and give inquisitors the power to pursue those who had made pacts with demons. In fact, the very first juridical application of this new mission is found in Ugolini's *Treatise on the Material of Heretics* (Ugolini was Clare's contemporary and a fellow citizen of Rimini). At the same time, churchmen began to see women as particularly susceptible to demonic possession. Learned churchmen might dabble dangerously in the dark arts necessary to conjure demons, but women were more likely to be seduced, in body or soul, by the lure of a simple pact with the devil and his demons. Thus Bernard Gui would label Margherita, Dolcino's companion, burned with him in 1307, as a *malefica*, a woman who does evil (*maleficia*) or black magic.

Clare stands at the crossroads of all these histories. Defiant in the face of denunciation, she is the unwilling heir to more than a century of heresy accusations in Rimini. She has the misfortune to be denounced just as efficient structures of repression are being finalized and just as wide-ranging constructions of a new kind of black magic are coming to dominate the minds of churchmen. The alchemy of this moment would lead, by the next century, to the creation of the figure that haunted early modern Europeans' imagination more than any other: the Witch.

CHAPTER 7

The Word of God

30. The saying of the apostle appeared with clarity in the servant of God, that *the word of God is living and powerful, more piercing than any knife, sharp to the point of dividing the spirit from the soul, and the joints from the marrow*.[1] Because in her, the servant of the Lord, this sweet speech brought back to life men almost dead, pierced with spiritual life hearts harder than stone, divided all things terrestrial from celestial, worldly from divine, animal from spiritual in human bodies,[2] as will appear from more examples below.

31. Among the other good works of Sister Clare, it happened that there was a certain noble countess who was a widow but who was poorly preserving the honesty of widowhood, giving herself instead to all pleasures and vanities; after having been visited and corrected by the servant of God, she was received in a religious manner among the number of her sisters. When she apologized for not taking a husband, because she could not find one worthy of her, the servant of God said to her: "Take that spouse who has no peer in nobility, no equal in his person, no rival in beauty, who cannot be approached in his wisdom, because he is God, because *he reigns* in glory *forever and ever*."[3] At these words, she was wondrously transformed, so that every desire and love that she once had for the world was converted to the Lord Jesus Christ. And she persevered perfectly in the habit and religion of the servant of Christ, ending her life in virtue and good conduct, and acquiring heavenly joy. And not only her, but her brother and all her family from then on lived in virtue and comported themselves honestly.[4]

32. At Mercatello, a castle of the Massa Trabaria, there was a lord named Bolognino who was ruling this castle like a tyrant.[5] He was visited by the servant of God, and stunned by her wisdom. And understanding that it was really Christ who spoke through her tongue,[6] he became a little brother (*fraticello*). And although he was very good-looking and very learned, he remained vanquished by her exhortations. Similarly, his very beautiful wife and his mother and his sister took the habit and the religion of the servant of God.

33. Similarly, another time, an educated young man, the son of a rich father, was passing through Rimini with some companions to go to the indulgence of the Ascension.[7] Hearing about the good reputation of Sister Clare, he went to visit her, to see her and hear her speak. And by her, he who until now could not leave behind the pleasures of the world, by her he was converted to Jesus Christ, with many of his friends and companions. But he, through grace and praiseworthy works, made the greatest advances of all, and finished his life in the grace of Jesus Christ.

34. Similarly, three great ladies, rich and noble, were returned from their public and disgraceful vanities to the *way of truth*[8] by the servant of God. Putting aside their worldly ornaments, and resplendent in their honest and moderate mode of life from that time on, in the grace of God they brought forth good fruit in their souls until the end of their lives.[9]

35. And to conclude this chapter on the spiritual and graceful speech of this Sister Clare, anyone who left for a far-off country, wasting his substance with lascivious women, was returned to his house and family by this servant of God.[10]

*   *   *

"The saying of the apostle appeared with clarity (*chiaramente*) in the servant of God." A bold opening, with a wink to the reader. The adverb translated as "with clarity" is one of our hagiographer's little jokes; *chiaramente* means "clearly," but the play on words suggests that *Chiara* (Clare) embodies the apostle Paul's statement that "the word of God is living and powerful."

Our hagiographer thus indicates that Clare is nothing less than a female apostle, even if Paul commanded that women "keep silence in the churches, for it is not permitted them to speak" (1 Cor. 14:34). One more paradox!

We have seen how Clare arrived at this point, taking a metaphor and brutally inscribing it on her body. For Clare, the impulse to chastise her tongue resulted not in a mental resolution to speak more carefully but in physically seizing her actual tongue with pincers, binding it fast, and suffering like this for a week. In Italian and Latin, the word for tongue, speech, and language is the same: *lingua*. Clare's tongue and speech were thus purified, and newly able to move, console, and bring peace to those who heard her. Now Clare, as the "servant of God," could indeed dare to take up the "living and powerful" word of God.

Clare's "visits" and "wisdom" inspire conversion after conversion: a widowed countess, along with her brother and family; the master of a castle; a rich, handsome, and educated young man, with his friends; and three wealthy noblewomen, not to mention all the prodigal sons who left home to waste their money on wanton women. Several of these episodes will be taken up and expanded in Chapter 10. Here, we can just note that, in each case, the conversion is collective. The power of Clare's words convinces not only her main interlocutor but his or her friends and relatives as well.

But the story of Clare's influence on the castellan of Mercatello hints at our hagiographer's ties with a controversial current of the Franciscan movement. We have already seen evidence (in Chapter 3) that our hagiographer is a friar, a member of the Franciscan Order. Here another slip of the pen suggests that his sympathies lie with the "Spiritual" Franciscans. In the decades following Francis's death (1226), two diverging tendencies emerged in the Order of Lesser Brothers. One insisted that Francis's absolute poverty was a model to be rigorously preserved in all its purity. The other was more moderate, willing to make commonsense compromises in order to pursue the practical work of preaching, hearing confessions, and administering the order. For decades, these were only tensions within the Franciscan brotherhood; but by the last quarter of the thirteenth century, they had burst into open conflict. The more radical wing of the order, inspired by the writing of the Franciscan theologian and philosopher Peter of John Olivi, gave the impossible quest for perfect poverty an apocalyptic twist, insisting that Franciscan poverty would play a crucial role in battling Antichrist and his allies in the "carnal" church before the Second Coming of Christ. These zealous brothers are generally referred to as "Spiritual" Franciscans, but were sometimes labeled as *Fraticelli* (singular: *fraticello*) by their opponents.

Things came to a head in 1294, with the election of a saintly hermit (Peter of Morrone) as Pope Celestine V, who, in turn, created the "Poor Hermits" as a home for some of the most ardent Spirituals, such as Angelo Clareno. But Celestine V renounced the papacy before the end of 1294 (Dante seems to attribute this "refusal" to "cowardice"; *Inferno* III, 59–60), and his successor, Boniface VIII (r. 1294–1303), had little patience for the Spirituals or *Fraticelli*. Figures such as Angelo Clareno and Ubertino of Casale were driven into opposition and exile, some in the March of Ancona, not far from Rimini. A whole group of penitent women moved in this orbit as well, including Margherita of Cortona, Angela of Foligno, and Clare of Montefalco (d. 1308), either as Franciscan tertiaries or as laywomen more loosely associated with Spiritual currents. During the pontificate of Clement V (r. 1305–1314), there were attempts at compromise, but the fiery pope John XXII (r. 1316–1332) came down squarely against the *Fraticelli* and their followers at the time of his election.

What does the story of Clare and "Lord Bolognino," who ruled a castle in the Massa Trabaria "like a tyrant," have to do with Franciscan controversies? Bolognino himself is an obscure figure. He was not a great lord but probably more of a small-time strongman in this mountainous, wooded area where the Romagna, Tuscany, the March of Ancona, and Umbria meet. And we have no idea how Clare came to find herself in this remote location. But however she may have encountered him, Clare converts this tyrant. "Stunned by her wisdom," this "very good-looking and very learned" man, with "his very beautiful wife and his mother and his sister, took the habit and the religion of the servant of God." As the hagiographer puts it, Lord Bolognino "became a little brother." The term he uses, however, is *fraticello*. The incident itself might have occurred before 1306. But our hagiographer is writing in the 1320s, after John XXII had forcefully condemned the *Fraticelli*—indeed, after a group of defiant Spirituals had been burned at the stake in Marseille in 1318 and as their followers were being hunted down. Only a Franciscan of Spiritual sympathies would have used this term in an approving way by this time. Indeed, in Chapter 6, when the hagiographer described the hostile preacher denouncing Clare for a second time, he had him call her *sorecta*, roughly a female equivalent of *fraticello*. The point is not that Clare was secretly a member of an organized sect resisting the church, but rather that our hagiographer moved in circles sympathetic to those persecuted by John XXII.

Was this backwoods "tyrant" Bolognino really "very learned"? We might have our doubts. But notably, "the son of a rich father," who was converted in the following episode, was also described as "an educated young man." And we remember that the friar who came to Clare to ask for advice in Chapter 6 was said to be "highly educated," too. By stressing the elite culture of Clare's converts, the hagiographer makes her victories more dramatic and underlines the force of her speech. Clare's life is a never-ending string of battles: against herself, against social and religious divisions, between the Gospel and the world, and between an inspired woman and educated men.

We have noted the ambiguity of the word *lingua* in Italian and Latin. When the hagiographer says that Bolognino understood that "it was really Christ who spoke *in la sua lingua*," does he mean "tongue," or "language"? And does he mean in "her" (Clare's) or in "his" tongue/language? The Italian could be translated either way. Was the tyrant stupefied to hear Christ speaking through Clare's tongue, or to hear Christ speaking in his language— that is, not in Latin but in the Italian of this region? Whatever the answer, the ambiguity is revealing. Another tension running through the text is between Latin and Italian; between the language of the clerics and the language of laypeople; between the "father" language (Latin) and "mother" language (Italian) that Dante, at the exactly same period, was praising as the *volgare illustre*.

CHAPTER 8

Visions of Community

36. Wanting to keep completely hidden the graces she was receiving from the Lord, Sister Clare went to receive communion at the church of San Matteo.[1] After taking communion, she felt a great emotion in her spirit, and it seemed to her as though a crown was being placed on her head,[2] with such a weight that for fifteen days, she could not turn her neck or her head. And wanting to return to her cell from which she had been taken away, she did not know how to move and could barely do so, and it seemed to her that she was carried to her cell by two angels, and it felt as if she never touched the ground.[3] And she recounted this, saying that something like this had happened before to a woman.[4] The next night, while she stood praying and inflicting very harsh punishments in her cell, since a sister named Benedetta of Cagli was there,[5] God showed with a marvelous vision[6] that he wanted to enlarge her narrow cell so that she could stay there with additional sisters. While they remained awake, suddenly a little majesty[7] and lamp were brought to her, which burned all the way to the house of a man named Lapo. There they stopped, and from there they were brought to the cell, where Sister Clare, putting her hands in front of her eyes, began to say, "Lord, what do you intend to do?" Her companions said, "Did you see that, what we saw?" And she answered, "Be quiet and don't say anything about it! Pray to God that he will show what we must do!" And thus it appears that this place was established by revelation and by miraculous signs.

37. As she grew in divine love from day to day, sometimes when Clare was speaking with certain women about divine and celestial things, she was rapt into ecstasy by an excess of love, and greatly raised up in such an excess of contemplation that, whatever was said or done around her, she did not perceive it or know about it.[8] And returning to herself, seeing the sun, the moon, or the stars, or even a child or something similar, she was filled with all sweetness and joy, considering the wonderful work of the Creator, to the point of being able to say: *Lord, you have given me delight in your doings, and in the works of your hands I shall rejoice.*[9] And thus the servant of God was made fruitful in good things; he was loved by her beyond all ordinary measure. And her mind was filled with infinite joy and raised up in the manifest and very truthful visions that the Lord showed her. But she did not rise up in pride on this account; in fact, with a querulous voice, she called herself a sinner, evil and unworthy of these graces.

38. God showed her, then, in a vision, that he wanted to enlarge her place, and that she ought to live with several sisters.[10] And this came into effect the next day because the landlord of the place and the land came to Clare, offering to sell it to her.[11] The holy woman,[12] confident in the Lord, accepted. And with the aid of God-fearing people, she satisfied it.[13] Thus she fixed this little house for herself and her sisters, where it appeared with great clarity that the order had been conceded to the blessed Clare by divine grace.

39. Now, finding herself content with the place, which she comfortably paid for with the help of God and the alms that were given to her, Clare gave infinite thanks to the high God for the benefits that she had received, and she decided to torment her life with the harshest tortures. The sisters, who had grown to the number of six, saw such sharp penitence in the blessed Clare that they—and, among others, Sister Druditia[14]—feared that she would not be able to endure it. And out of charity, they tried to impede her, to some degree, to give her a little rest. Thus, near evening, they enclosed her in the little cell, and they locked the little door securely from the outside. Then, going to see her a little later, they found her in her usual spot at the wall, singing psalms and other offices—she did not rest, because she did not

remain still—all night and up until morning. And the little door remained locked, just as they had left it.

* * *

Before following our hagiographer any further, it is worth pausing to recap the structure of his narrative so far. The first two chapters take Clare from her birth around 1260, through her marriages and worldly life, to her conversion in the 1290s. Chapters 3 through 7 describe Clare's life over the next two decades. Chapter 4 relates her exile in Urbino, and Chapters 3, 5, 6, and 7 are thematic, focusing on Clare's penitence (Chapter 3), speech (Chapter 5), brush with heresy (Chapter 6), and success in converting those around her (Chapter 7). These chapters certainly relate many biographical details and contain other themes, such as Clare's care for the poor, which connect one chapter to the next. But within this section of the *Life*, our hagiographer has primarily chosen to arrange his work thematically.

He had a practical reason for adopting this strategy. We can imagine him working from the testimonies of Clare's female companions, forming a kind of hagiographic team (just as Thomas of Celano had based his Latin *Legend* of St. Clare of Assisi on the testimonies of her sisters during her canonization process in 1255). Druditia reported everything that she could, but she had not always been by her sister's side. The women who later congregated around Clare heard her recount the most dramatic moments of her own life, like modern parables, but haphazardly, without any clear chronological order. The hagiographer's only option was to sort these anecdotes into thematic strands. In this way, he could shape his heroine's experience into an ideal trajectory: sin leads to repentance; public teaching spawns accusations of heresy; but success in converting others ultimately legitimates Clare's actions. Our hagiographer has made the best of the available material.

Beginning in Chapter 8, a new dynamic drives the text. A third stage of Clare's life now begins (after her marriages and her solitary existence as a penitent), as a small community of women takes shape around her. The hagiographer's witnesses no longer report mere hearsay; these sisters have lived side by side with their founder and spiritual mother for years. Thus their stories take on a new precision in relating what they see and hear. Often, these women

themselves lurk around the edges of the episodes that they relate. Their rec-
ollections begin to speak more clearly for themselves. We need only add our
comments at the margins, the way medieval scholars inscribed their glosses
around the text of the Bible.

*   *   *

Clare went to receive communion at San Matteo, the church of the Humiliati
in Rimini. The Humiliati were penitent laypeople with a controversial history
to match Clare's. Their movement began in the later twelfth century, part
of the same apostolic impulse that would eventually produce the mendicant
orders. In Milan and other cities of Lombardy, these men and women gathered
together to live in simplicity, often making a living as wool-workers, refusing to swear oaths or bear arms, and dedicating themselves to prayers, fasts,
and pious exhortation. Many were married, though some favored celibacy. Their
early history was dogged by suspicion. In 1184, the Humiliati were condemned
by the church (along with the followers of Waldes of Lyon, similarly inspired
laypeople seeking an apostolic life). But in 1201, Pope Innocent III welcomed
the Humiliati back into the church, organizing them into three groups: clerics; laypeople living in a semimonastic style; and married men and women
remaining in the world. During the thirteenth century, the first two groups
tended to fuse, while the third faced competition from other penitent groups,
including the mendicant third orders. A Humiliati community had taken
shape in Rimini by 1261, favored by the Commune because of its utility for
the wool industry. By 1299, however, this community was entirely made up
of female members. San Matteo, the church given to them, was outside Clare's
neighborhood. Thus she may have gone there to receive communion in the
company of this group of like-minded women. But was she entirely determined "to keep completely hidden the graces she was receiving from the
Lord"? We might wonder. Not establishing a church for her own community meant that Clare would have to appear in public to hear Mass, and so
attract wider attention in the city.

Our hagiographer chooses this setting to open his chapter about Clare's
bold move to found a larger community of her own. Alluding to the Humiliati helps him to suggest that penitent women such as those gathered at San
Matteo could find an accepted place in Rimini. The process would not be easy.

After taking communion at San Matteo, Clare feels that she has been symbolically crowned; but rather than a triumph, this crowning literally weighs on her so heavily that only angelic intervention allows her to return to her cell. Clare herself is careful to recount this tale to her sisters, later, as a dramatic prelude to the moment of their community's foundation. She recalls that "something like this had happened before to a woman." How should we interpret this enigmatic allusion? Was she referring to some local figure who had undergone a similar experience? Cardinal Giacomo Colonna, for example, had seen his holy sister Margherita (c. 1255–1280) carried by two angels as a sign that she should embrace a life of virginity. This vision had occurred around 1272, when the cardinal was visiting the Franciscans of nearby Bologna. Still, it seems unlikely that any such recent event was on Clare's mind. Was the "woman" the Virgin Mary, increasingly represented in mosaics, frescoes, and altarpieces as crowned by her son amid a host of angels? Or Mary Magdalene, said in her solitary retirement to have been transported by angels each day to a mountaintop? Ascension is a recurring theme in ancient and medieval iconography, drawing on the classic theme of apotheosis (the elevation of a mortal to heaven). In this case, the crown and angels strongly suggest the influence of some such image before which Clare would have prayed and meditated, perhaps in the very church of San Matteo.

The next night, back in her cell, while "inflicting very harsh punishments" on herself, Clare has a vision. But already she is not alone; Benedetta, a sister from Cagli, is by her side. Indeed, the hagiographer hesitates between singular and plural onlookers; a moment later, he will refer to Clare's "companions" who were present. This collective experience is the point of the marvelous vision that Clare now experiences: God wants her to live "with additional sisters." The sign of God's will is "a little majesty" (*maiestadecta*) and lighted lamps. A "majesty," or *maestà*, refers to a representation of the Virgin "in majesty"—that is, seated on a throne with the Christ child in her lap and surrounded by angels. They could be imposing altar decorations, but when painted on small, portable wooden tablets, they could aid private devotion at home. In this case, "burning lamps" lit the way as the miraculous vision "was carried" to the nearby home of a man named Lapo, stopping there as a sign. The whole scene masks the wrenching decision at the heart of this chapter—should Clare leave her little cell to enlarge her community? Would such a step fulfill or betray her original calling as a solitary penitent? In this telling, the decision is made for her; Clare could hardly refuse the divine will that had been so clearly made manifest by the "revelation and miraculous signs." Recourse to such visions and signs also has a long history rooted in classical and medieval literatures, mythologies, and religions.

Still, the hagiographer hesitates. A flurry of visions holds the moment in suspense; "sometimes" when speaking with other women, Clare would be "rapt into ecstasy" and lose contact with the reality around her. Clare is filled with joy by these "excesses" of love and contemplation; yet she calls herself an evil and unworthy sinner. The hagiographer seems to stall for time, reluctant to advance his narrative. The content of Clare's visions—the sun, the moon, the stars, a child—merely repeats what he has already related in Chapter 5.

Finally, the tension breaks. The author repeats a sentence he has written just a few lines before, stressing with this repetition the significance of the divine vision which grants Clare permission to proceed: "God showed her then, in a vision, that he wanted to enlarge her place, and that she ought to live with several sisters." This comes about when "the landlord" (*patrone*), presumably Lapo, offers to sell his house to Clare. She accepts. No sooner has she paid, with alms she has gathered, than a group of six sisters appears around her. The story is simple, but the hagiographer's unease is palpable. If Lapo sold the house, then Clare bought it. And if she bought it, that means she amassed money. Is the Lord's work really carried out through cash transactions?

All rhetorical stops are pulled out to paper over the awkwardness. The moment that Clare agrees to the purchase is the one and only time in the entire text that she is called a "holy" or "saintly woman" (*sancta donna*). Only three times in the whole text, and once in the title itself, is she called "blessed" (*beata*). Two of these instances appear just at this point. The stench of money is covered up with the perfume of sanctity. And Clare herself instantly decides "to torment her life with the harshest tortures," as if atoning for her sin. Her sisters—including her biological sister Druditia—are forced to lock her up for her own protection.

To this point, it has been Clare's separation from the normal social life of the city that has won her attention, whether approving or disapproving. At certain moments, her strident asceticism and outlandish audacity have caused scandal; but slowly, a group of unquiet souls has been drawn to her, searching for answers to their own spiritual uncertainties. Wanting to flee the world, they form a little community. As early as Chapters 3 and 4, our hagiographer has gotten ahead of himself and referred several times to Clare's "sisters"; but before Chapter 8, only Druditia (her biological as well as spiritual sister) has been mentioned by name. Now we meet Sister Benedetta of Cagli; and in Chapter 9, we will be introduced to Sisters Amata and Agnes. Another Sister Clare (not the same as our heroine) pops up in Chapter 10, and Sisters Amata and Agnes reappear, along with Sister Agnesina, in Chapter 11. In Chapter 12, we find not only Sisters Agnes, Amata, and Druditia but also Viola of Gubbio, Nicoluccia, and Catherina. Altogether, nine sisters are referred to by name, several of them more than once. After Druditia, it is Agnes and Amata who seem to be our hagiographer's most frequent informants. We might guess that most of these women were from Rimini proper; but evidently, Clare's reputation drew women from farther afield as well, since Cagli, still in the March of Ancona, is about a ninety-five-kilometer (sixty-mile) journey south of Rimini, while Gubbio is another thirty kilometers (nineteen miles) south into Umbria. Both these cities are on the road from Rimini to Assisi (via Pesaro). This is no coincidence, as we shall see in Chapter 10.

These women sought to flee the world, but the very process of group formation inevitably ties them back to the society that they sought to leave behind. Now the holy woman is torn! Her success reassures her that God approves of her actions. But at the same time, it torments her, since her solitary communion with God is drowned out by the chatter of her admiring circle. For a suffering saint, even success produces only a redoubled round of anguish. Clare feels remorse for having left her roofless cell. So when her sisters lock her in to their new dwelling—the very dwelling that Clare has decided God wants her to inhabit—she miraculously escapes, like a holy Houdini, and is found back "in her usual spot at the wall," singing psalms all night.

For the founder of a religious community, installation is always both a reward and a sacrifice. But in this case, it again places Clare at the heart of a raging debate. In referring to Lapo's house, the hagiographer uses the Italian word *loco* (modern Italian: *luogo*), meaning "place." It is the strict equivalent of the Latin *locus*, the term that Francis of Assisi used to designate the houses of the Lesser Brothers. Our Franciscan hagiographer has once more dropped us squarely into a Franciscan controversy. Francis wished for his brothers to possess nothing. This was fine when he had twelve companions; it did not

work so well with an order of five thousand friars by the 1220s. If these
brothers were going to preach (and therefore study), a compromise with the
ideal of absolute poverty would be necessary. The brothers needed books
and the basic necessities of life. Pope Gregory IX first proposed that the friars'
goods would be considered to belong to well-wishing friends of the order;
legally, Franciscans would possess nothing. Innocent IV solidified this fiction
in 1245 by declaring that the papacy itself owned all the houses and goods
held by the order; the brothers had only their "use." These were exactly the
compromises that led to the divergence between zealous "Spiritual" and more
moderate "Community" wings of the order. As we have seen, by the early
fourteenth century this split had devolved into open warfare.

Clare embodies both sides of this debate at once, trapped by the impossibility of reconciling two contradictory imperatives. She has left behind the
world with its wealth and luxury, and God, in a vision, has assured her of
divine sanction for her project. But to acquire a house for her companions,
she must raise cash. Now it is no longer a question of begging for bread to
support the poor. She needs money, plain and simple. And once the real-
estate transaction is complete, she is saddled with what we might call the
social responsibilities of a home owner, no matter how modest that home
might be. Lapo had been referred to as the *patrone* of the *loco*, the landlord
or patron of the place. Now it is Clare who is the patron or owner of the
property, by virtue of her all-cash purchase. But she is only too aware of
Francis's admonition that money soils everything that it touches. Clare's
moment of foundation is anything but a relief.

The new house is only a stone's throw from her old cell, in the eastern
section of the city, overlooking the sea, in a neighborhood as far as possible
from the city hall and the cathedral (see Map 2, in Chapter 5). This neighborhood is said by our hagiographer (in Chapter 6) to be "filled with evil
people who committed adultery and murder." Why did Clare gravitate to this
neighborhood in the first place? For one thing, it was the refuge of outcasts
and newcomers, the poor and the marginal. Indeed, in Chapter 6, we have
seen that this area was referred to as the neighborhood of the patarines, and
had suffered destruction in the 1250s as a result. Thus it was not a coincidence
that it was also the neighborhood where the house and church of St. Francis had
stood since the friars arrived in Rimini in 1257, because the Franciscans
sought both to help the poor and to fight against heresy. Clare's first visions,

leading her to penitent conversion, had come in this church. In all likelihood, the accusations of heresy had emanated from friars there, too. Eventually, her hagiographer would emerge from this community. Still, Clare's new house is equidistant from the Franciscan community and the Dominican church where she received the Eucharist at the end of Chapter 4.

Clare's spirituality and inspiration rarely stray far from Francis of Assisi. But in this instance, Clare seems to betray the *Poverello's* underlying ideals. When the Commune of Assisi had wanted to build a house for Francis's early companions, he clambered atop the roof and began to tear it apart, shingle by shingle. Clare, by contrast, desires a home for her community, at all costs. If achieving this end means dirtying her hands with money, so be it. In so doing, she arrives at a solution related to the one accepted by the other Clare—Clare of Assisi—decades earlier. The virgin of Assisi would probably have liked to have followed the friars and to have begged door-to-door, without possessing anything. But Francis, like most churchmen, assumed that religious women should be enclosed behind firm walls. So Clare of Assisi and her sisters had to accept a certain form of stability and enclosure. Still, Clare of Assisi insisted in her rule that the Poor Sisters would possess nothing but the land on which their monastery stood. Both Clares found a practical compromise between their ideals and the specific burdens that medieval mentalities placed on women's shoulders. Our Clare remains torn, even by this compromise.

CHAPTER 9

From Intuition to Institution

40. Now, having heard several times that our Lord Jesus Christ sweated blood while in prayer[1]—signifying the sufferings and tortures that his whole body had to pour out—and that this same Lord was struck with slaps, his face fouled with spit and his side pierced with the lance, and his hands fixed to the wood of the cross with sharp nails and a crown of spiky thorns fixed to his head, and then, in the end, when he said, "*I thirst*," bile and vinegar were given to him to drink,[2] Sister Clare wanted to make herself a perfect imitator of this suffering and other martyrdoms, through every pain, for the salvation of her life. So on Good Friday, the day on which Jesus Christ was crucified and endured such pain, early that morning she hired two ruffians.[3] After having promptly visited the bishop's cathedral of Rimini—which is called Santa Colomba, patron saint of the church—alongside the palace where the public square of the Commune is situated, she then ordered that they tie her hands turned behind her back, with tight bonds. The said ruffians led her by a cord around her neck over to a stone column and tied her there, as she wanted. And there she stayed, tied up in this way, until Saturday at nones. Then, once the offices had been recited, they untied her from the column. With her hands still bound, the halter at her neck, dressed in her underclothes, begging people to beat her cruelly with branches or their bare hands, she went around to the churches of the city and suburbs, very carefully searching out each one. Then she went back to her cell, greatly afflicted.[4] And every single year on those days, she tormented her body in the same way. She burned with such a fervent love for our Lord's Passion that nothing

was enough for her chastisement and correction. Finally, when her sisters forced her to stop this practice, she gave up summoning the ruffians and carrying out such works of suffering so publicly. A few days later, conferring with her sisters, she told them that out of all the vexing martyrdoms she had suffered in her life, that was the most grievous. But God's help, from which all rewards and victories come, sustained her.

41. At this time, she received gracious permission from my lord Cardinal Napoleone,[5] who had come as legate to the March [of Treviso], that members of religious orders could celebrate the whole office in its entirety in the place of Sister Clare. His most reverend lordship consented to her worthy prayers; receiving this gracious permission gave Sister Clare joy beyond belief. Then she hurried to find a cleric of good habits, filled with goodness, who would be for her an ark of counsel and light and a mirror for her life; for this woman knew and had experienced that *if the blind lead the blind* down the road, *both fall into the ditch.*[6] And after she found such a religious man, he began to celebrate the divine office in the said church as it should be done, following the proper order.[7]

42. And although she had the habit and custom of confessing continually and taking communion every feast of our Lady and of our Lord and of the apostles as well as every Wednesday and Friday, nonetheless, once the religious man came, she confessed with great contemplation every evening, not unthinkingly but with reverence and fear, pronouncing herself unworthy to be an innkeeper for such a king, in the holy memory of our Redeemer. And from a late hour until nones the next day, she would remain fervently in prayer, with tears and repentance, full of every pain, and recalling all her sins. And remembering the Passion of the Lord in this way, she was marvelously transfigured.

43. Now, seeing Sister Clare in such ardent contemplation, Jesus Christ inspired her and her companions to refrain from speaking very much, and to observe silence. She remained for fifteen days, such that her tongue could not enunciate the least speech with others but only with herself, so tongue-tied was she. And it happened to her many times that for several days, she was completely unable to enunciate

normal speech clearly, as if she were without a tongue. And from then on, all her life she kept a marvelous silence, especially from midnight to nones of the following day. And even if she had wished, her tongue could not have expressed anything. Later, God miraculously restored the organs of her lost voice. And the sisters fully understood this silence, as much before as after, because it was known and manifest to all those who wanted to know the true practices of this Sister Clare, as reported by Sister Amata and Sister Agnes,[8] among other sisters who would not deserve to be passed over in silence but who were afraid to remain in the church, and especially the youngest. Sister Clare kept up these contemplations and silences with such great fervor that to sin against the divine excellence would have been like a wound from a sharp dagger.[9]

44. By her comportment, with her voice and her tears, she testified to this, and always prayed to God that he would raise her to the path of the true light and the clarity of truth[10] and that he would correct her crimes and misdeeds, because many are the wicked ways of women.[11] So she prayed to God, crying and praying, that she and her companions might return to the path of clarity. In this way, she led her sisters to good works and penance, clothing them and finding alms for them, with great effort, from the city. And she gloried in the Lord in all things.[12]

* * *

Clare's Christ is not the triumphant conqueror of earlier Romanesque portals: slapped, spit upon, pierced with the lance, nailed to the cross, crowned with thorns, he is the Man of Sorrows, broken and bleeding, the suffering Christ that St. Francis had imitated to the point of absorbing the marks of the stigmata into his own body. The extraordinary story that begins Chapter 9 is Clare's *imitatio Christi* (the practice of imitating or copying Jesus's example) but filtered through her imitation of Francis. Once, when Francis had moderated his fasting to recover from an illness, his sense of guilt drove him to enter a church, in front of all his fellow citizens, where he ordered his brothers to bind him to a pillar, with a rope around his neck. In recounting this anecdote, the Franciscan minister general, Bonaventure, cautioned that such extreme acts of penance were to be admired rather than imitated. Nevertheless, others took up this penitential path. In 1260, waves of penance (perhaps driven by apocalyptic fears) swept through Perugia and other Italian cities, with citizens processing through the streets whipping themselves until they bled. Such collective acts of public flagellation became part of the late medieval urban landscape, reappearing in the face of any new cataclysm.

Indeed, on January 25, 1308, a powerful earthquake shook Rimini's walls, towers, and homes. According to the report of a contemporary witness (added to a manuscript copy of the Statutes of the Commune of Rimini), "Fear produced such devotion that all the inhabitants of the city, from the highest to the lowest, did penance, confessing their sins and whipping themselves day and night for nearly a month, visiting all the churches of the city and begging for God's mercy." These processions took place barely a year after events recounted in this chapter (as we shall see). We might wonder what role Clare played in popularizing such intensely penitent practices in her native city.

Clare's scandalous actions stand out for their spectacular violence as well as their careful planning. It took foresight to hire "two ruffians" early in the morning of Good Friday; it took a desire for public spectacle to choose a location in the piazza (public square) outside the cathedral of Santa Colomba for her two-day display of penitent suffering. We might even call this an interactive performance, involving onlookers from across Rimini as Clare invited them to "beat her cruelly with branches" as she was led through the city and its suburbs. "Visiting all the churches" of Rimini, just as the flagellants of 1308 would do, was a theatrical production in the most literal sense.

By reenacting the sacred drama of the Passion, moving through urban space to create a devout commemoration of Christ's suffering on earth, Clare turns the streets of Rimini into a stage for public performance. As with the teaching that led to her denunciation as a heretic, Clare is here engaged in an audacious display. She makes herself the center of attention, "dressed in her underclothes," calling on her fellow citizens to join in her penitence. In 1260, the women of Perugia had limited themselves to flagellation "in their chambers"; only in 1349, after the onset of the Black Death, nearly half a century after Clare's adoption of this Good Friday ritual, would women begin to routinely display this kind of public penance. Clare's exhibition is nothing short of scandalous, implying that, in Rimini, Christ had been reincarnated as a woman on the anniversary of his crucifixion.

Our hagiographer tries to balance the highly public nature of Clare's actions by emphasizing her eventual retreat "back to her cell." This reference to her "cell" indicates that Clare had begun this annual practice while she still lived a solitary existence. But it continued "every single year," until finally, the "sisters" of her new community persuaded her to cease "carrying out such works of suffering so publicly." Clare agrees, with great reluctance, to put an end to her annual ritual, now that she is the leader of a more settled community. The "martyrdom" for Clare is not the suffering; it is consenting to give it up.

*   *   *

"At this time," Clare received a crucial mark of ecclesiastical favor from Cardinal Napoleone Orsini. The Orsini were one of the most powerful families of Rome, part of the small circle of Roman clans that dominated the secular offices of Rome and the ecclesiastical honors dispensed by the papacy. Napoleone was born around 1263 (making him about the same age as Clare) and had been named a cardinal in 1288. He was thus a powerful prince of the church, with his promotion at such a young age due less to any precocious display of personal merit than to the traditional workings of Roman patronage. Cardinal Napoleone could scheme as shrewdly as anyone else at the curia, but he was also capable of principled positions. He had favored the election of Celestine V in 1294 and joined the opposition to Boniface VIII. He even opposed his more senior kinsman, Cardinal Matteo Orsini, in supporting the election of Clement V in 1305. As a reward, Clement appointed Cardinal Napoleone as papal legate (official papal representative) to the March of Treviso, Tuscany, the Romagna, Sardinia, Corsica, and Genoa, from 1306 to 1308. It was in this capacity that Napoleone visited Rimini in December 1306. For once, we can assign a firm date to a moment in Clare's *Life*, since it was surely on this visit that the cardinal granted his "gracious permission" that "members of religious orders could celebrate the whole office in its entirety in the place of Sister Clare."

Napoleone Orsini's favor ties Clare of Rimini to a wider circle of like-minded women and men in the orbit of the Spiritual Franciscans. Napoleone was a sincere admirer of Francis of Assisi—even sponsoring a chapel in the lower basilica of San Francesco in Assisi—and a supporter of those who tried to uphold his legacy. In 1294, Celestine V had charged him with protecting the "Poor Hermits," Angelo Clareno's group that had broken with the Franciscan Order to try to live up to Francis's ideal of poverty. In 1306, Cardinal Napoleone was not only still supporting the controversial Clareno but had also taken on as his personal chaplain Ubertino of Casale, a similar figure for the Spirituals of Tuscany. Napoleone Orsini thus protected some of the fieriest proponents of the Spiritual cause, in the years leading up to John XXII's determined effort to stamp out these rebellious friars.

Well before that final showdown, however, Cardinal Napoleone and his chaplain Ubertino showed particular favor for a number of Italian holy women. As early as the 1280s, Ubertino had been close to Margherita of Cortona, directly inspired by Angela of Foligno (as he wrote himself in his *Tree of Life* in 1305), and in conversation with Clare of Montefalco. Napoleone and Ubertino then worked together to promote the memory of these women. After Margherita of Cortona died in 1297, her confessor Giunta Bevegnati wrote her *Life*, which records that Ubertino "preached" about how the cardinal legate Napoleone Orsini had kept a copy of this text with him at the papal curia for months and had given it his solemn approval before Ubertino and other friars on February 15, 1308. On August 17 in that same year, Clare of Montefalco died; in November, Napoleone Orsini was sent to Rome to validate the miraculous signs that had been found inscribed on her heart.

Margherita of Cortona, Clare of Montefalco, and Angela of Foligno were all penitents and tertiaries. Margherita and Angela joined the Franciscan Third Order, Clare the Augustinian. But all three were firmly in the orbit of the Spiritual Franciscans and embraced a spirituality centered on poverty, the Eucharist, and imitation of the suffering Christ. Napoleone Orsini, with his chaplain Ubertino of Casale, was engaged in a concerted effort to promote the profiles of these women dedicated to evangelical renewal of the church. In this light, Cardinal Orsini's favor for Clare of Rimini at the end of 1306 appears anything but random. Here was one more ardent penitent, balanced on the thin line between sanctity and heresy. She had suffered her share of suspicion but recovered her good standing in the community. When Clare approached "his most reverend lordship" with "her worthy prayers," how could he refuse? Where the upper echelons of the ecclesiastical hierarchy seemed rife with complacency, salvation could be sought through the example of unlearned women who exemplified the original simplicity of the ideals lived by Jesus Christ.

As always, it would be a mistake to underestimate our hagiographer's skill in crafting his narrative. The scandal of Clare's public Good Friday performances is immediately wiped away by the cardinal legate's support. The previous paragraph could have left a lingering image of the half-naked Clare led bleeding through the streets. But suddenly, a lord of the church enters the scene to consent to "her worthy prayers." The effect is, once again, to record Clare's notoriety and preserve her example as a fool for Christ, while also muffling the echoes of her actions.

With this new permission to have members of religious orders celebrate the divine office at her fledgling female community, Clare rushes to find an appropriate priest, who "began to celebrate the divine office in the said church as it should be done, following the necessary order," as spelled out in the (presumably Franciscan) breviary. Up to now, the "place" purchased from Lapo has seemed to be just a little house. Suddenly, in this passage, we find ourselves in the presence of a church! We have to wait until 1367 for a document that gives it a name: Santa Maria dell'Annunciazione (by 1457, it had become known as Santa Maria degli Angeli). But already in a manuscript from 1322, we find a revealing reference (see Figure 1). The manuscript is a French commentary on the Gospels, Acts of the Apostles, and Apocalypse, made for Ferrantino Malatesta, ruler of Rimini, together with his uncle Pandolfo, from 1317 to 1326. The text was completed by the scribe Pierre of Cambrai on January 23, 1322; then, 234 charmingly delicate miniatures were added by Neri of Rimini. But such artists did not merely consult their own inspiration; they took direction from their patrons. In this case, we find a marginal note, copied out by Pierre (in Latin, since he was French and the painter was Italian) to indicate what Neri should paint: "Here is found Jesus seated on a throne (*cathedra*) among the doctors, and there is a temple; and it should be painted as it is in the church of Sister Clare." So by 1322, evidently still within the lifetime of "Sister Clare," not only had a little monastic compound taken shape on Lapo's "place," but the church there was already so well adorned as to inspire artistic imitation. The divine office could indeed be carried out there "as it should be done." This was the implication of Cardinal Napoleone's intervention: to bring formality and stability to what had been an informal, unstable arrangement.

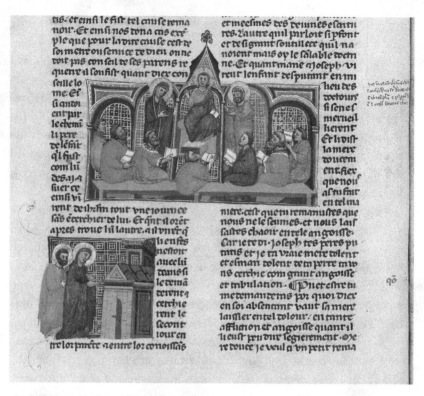

Figure 1. Marginal reference to "the church of Sister Clare" in a manuscript of 1322. Text in the right margin reads: *Hic inveniunt Ihesum sedentem in cathedra inter doctores et est ibi templum et pingatur sicut est in ecclesia sororis Clare* ("Here is found Jesus seated on a throne among the doctors, and there is a temple; and it should be painted as it is in the church of Sister Clare"). Vatican City, Biblioteca Apostolica Vaticana, MS Urb. lat. 11 (*Expositiones omnium evangeliorum lingua gallica*), fol. 170v. Used by permission of the Biblioteca Apostolica Vaticana.

Our hagiographer continues his pattern: controversy leads to a legitimating moment of institutionalization; but institutionalization is followed by unease. Do order and approval mean a cooling of fervor? The *Life* is at great pains to stress the opposite. Clare had confessed, prayed, and taken communion frequently before; but now, she seems nearly frenzied in her efforts. Again, her tongue seems to be at the center of all her struggles. Whereas in Chapter 5, Clare's efforts to discipline this organ had taken a painfully literal turn, here she has such difficulty speaking that it is "as if she were without a tongue." But behind Clare's self-reproach and tears, the hagiographer sketches the unwritten rule of life that will guide Clare's community: regular attendance at the divine office, a rhythm of confession and communion, the obligation of silence, works of penance, norms of clothing, and alms-seeking. Rather than writing out a formal rule, Clare legislates through example, insisting that salvation rests on the most scrupulous adherence to these practices. Just as Francis was the "form of the Minors" (*forma Minorum*), Clare embodies the form of life (*forma vite*) of her sisters. Clare does not ground an insistence on silence in citations from the Psalms, as in the Benedictine Rule. In Clare's mental universe, the obligation of silence is demonstrated by her personal story and singular experience, authenticated by the marvels that emerge in her wake.

What kind of religious life would come out of this unwritten rule? Clare's ideal seems to have been the "mixed" life, which brought together active and contemplative elements. Just as Clare had been doing ever since her early experiments in Urbino, her sisters now devote themselves to prayer, silence, repentance, and meditation, from the evening right through the next day. Afternoons were reserved for "good works and penance," though Clare alone would go into the streets to seek out clothes and provisions for her sisters.

More specifically, were Clare's sisters formally tied to any approved order? In the eighteenth century, at the time of Clare's beatification, Italian scholars engaged in a long dispute over whether her community could be identified as part of the Franciscan Order. Clearly, the sisters were not enclosed nuns of the Order of St. Clare (the so-called Second Order). But were they Franciscan tertiaries? The short answer must be no. Pope Nicholas IV's bull *Supra montem* standardized the practices of the Franciscan "Third Order" in 1289, and a close examination makes clear that the specifics of Clare's fasts, confessions, and attendance at Mass do not accord with those legislative standards. Francis of Assisi was certainly Clare's most immediate inspiration. But in Urbino, she had placed herself under a secular canon's protection; and in Rimini, she frequented the Dominican church as well as the Franciscan. As always, Clare resists easy categorization.

This chapter may offer a further clue about the origins of Clare's ties to our hagiographer. We have seen (in Chapter 3) that he was surely a Franciscan, and we have picked up hints (in Chapter 7) that he must have favored the Spiritual wing of the order. How did he come to be so closely linked to his subject? The most likely possibility is that he acted as Clare's confessor. When Cardinal Napoleone granted permission for "members of religious orders" to celebrate the divine office in Clare's "place," Clare had to seek out "a cleric of good habits" to fill this role. Where would she have turned to find such a cleric? At the neighboring Franciscan house, almost certainly. In turn, this friar, "filled with goodness . . . an ark of counsel and light, and a mirror for her life," became her confessor, to whom "she confessed with great contemplation every evening." Was this confessor the same man as the Franciscan who would write Clare's *Life* two decades later? It seems possible—though, in that case, his glowing self-descriptions ("filled with goodness . . . an ark of counsel and light") would be rather immodest. Perhaps we should imagine that this first friar gave way to a successor. In any case, this newly formalized relationship with a Franciscan confessor must have only increased Clare's curiosity about Francis, his order, its past, and the debates and controversies that it was currently experiencing.

*   *   *

Human history moves by fits and starts, through transgressions and innovations. In her humble way, Clare of Rimini moved history along by defying expectations. A transgression only has meaning when measured against an established tradition. Clare's reenactment of the Passion of Christ recalled the practice of going from station to station (church to church) in Rome at Lent, as well as the "Way of the Cross" recently instituted by Franciscans at Jerusalem. She can even be seen as a pioneer in the staging of Good Friday Passion plays, which were just starting to take shape in Italy and elsewhere in this era. Yet in these ways, she was pushing the boundaries of tradition more than transgressing norms. Clare's great transgression, in fact, was simple: every year on Good Friday in Rimini, it was a *woman* who took on the role of Christ. This reversal of gender at the most emotional moment of the Christian calendar was really too much for her contemporaries. Clare could easily have been condemned again, with dire consequences.

But thanks to Napoleone Orsini's intervention, a kind of deal is reached: Clare renounces her annual reenactments and receives the cardinal's approval for her community. That community now has a firm location, the support of at least one cleric/confessor, and an unwritten rule incarnated in Clare. Her sisters are encouraged to follow a moderated form of her example, though Clare herself still goes out into the streets to beg for food, like an echo, in a minor mode, of her earlier transgressions. But a change has taken place. As the pioneering sociologist Max Weber would have framed it, Clare's charism has given way to a process of "routinization." Or, to borrow from the title of an illuminating book by Théophile Desbonnets, her intuition has been rewarded by institutionalization.

CHAPTER 10

An Apostle on the Road

45. A certain poor little woman (*poverella donna*) came to Sister Clare. She had only a little daughter, who deeply wished to enter the religion[1] of the Santuccia sisters, outside the gate of Rimini.[2] But they did not want to accept her if she could not pay the great sum of money requested. Hearing this, Sister Clare hurried to visit the said sisters. And with humble and sweet prayers, she wished to correct and amend the greed of these women. Taught by the doctrine of the Gospel, she reminded them that if we give small gifts in this life to the needy and the poor, we will receive them back a hundredfold or more.[3] And she wonderfully informed them about the charity of our Lord, and about his life, conduct, and examples. She made them feel so ashamed, and she admonished them, so that eventually the poor little young woman was accepted into their company without any payment or gifts, with a large and noble company of citizens [looking on]. [Clare's] speech was of such virtue and force that nothing could be refused to her.

46. Now there was a peasant woman there, who had a wounded, incurable, and cancerous breast, which had swollen to the size of a little pumpkin. So the abbess and the other sisters begged Sister Clare, insistently and kneeling on the ground, that she might wish to place her hand on the breast, out of charity. And when she had done this, the breast suddenly shrank and was returned to its original state of health. The abbess, sisters, and other women who were there, clearly seeing this and rising from their knees, showed her the breast restored to health.[4] And [Clare] said: "Recognize the graces that the most kind Creator has granted to you!" and she returned to her cell.

47. At this time, there was a certain noble countess who was very vain and pompous in the works of this world, considering the true life as though it were nothing.[5] Although she was a widow, she wore noble and rich fabrics, lined with vair,[6] with a silver belt at her waist. Riding with her brother, hunting and birding through the woods, valleys, and mountaintops, she ventured everywhere, far from any path of honesty. And while she was in such danger, a sister, who was named Clare, spoke with the said blessed Sister Clare and said to her, "Why don't you visit my lady the countess, who is caught up in such great vanity and observes no sign of widowhood in word or deed?" So Sister Clare came to her, wanting the holy works of God to increase and the countess to love God with all her heart. And after a little while, [Sister Clare] said to her, "My lady the countess, you are very vain. Why do you not take a husband? It will be more convenient for you, and your bad reputation will diminish and disappear." The countess replied, "I have not yet been able to find someone I like and who would be pleasing to me." And the servant of God said to her, "Then take eternal God, who is more noble than you, and of more generous parentage and family, who neither grows old nor becomes deformed or ugly over time, who will reign forever and ever." With these words, like arrows to the heart of the countess, Clare struck her and pierced her heart all at once. As though wounded by a sharp dagger, [the countess] fell into the arms of the servant of God, with a great flow of tears, saying in a high and loud voice that with all her heart she sought such a Lord as her spouse. At this noise, her brother and all her family came running and gathered around her and asked her what had happened to her. Sister Clare quickly departed. And a few days later, the countess asked for her, through [the other] Sister Clare. When she arrived, with scissors in her own hands, she cut the loveliness of [the countess's] most luminous hair down to her scalp, dressed her in a cilice[7] and a grayish brown habit, and belted her with a contemptible cord. The countess remained for many years in a religious habit, with good works and virtuous words.[8] Then, when death arrived, separating her soul from her body, she reposed in the Lord. And well instructed by the countess's good conduct, her brother and all her family lived virtuously.

48. A certain poor woman was seeking alms across the city, since her husband was in prison. And since she could not find enough money to satisfy the Commune, her husband's hand was to be cut off.[9] So the servant of God, moved by fervent charity, went to the piazza of the Commune in hurried haste. She climbed up on a large stone and began to ask if anyone wanted to buy her, in order to buy back a hand that was to be cut off. This became known across the city, and the Malatesta lords heard about what such a little woman (*donnicella*) had done.[10] They summoned her and said to her: "To you, mercy has been granted." And thus [the husband] was freed from prison without any hindrance.

49. At this time, Sister Clare headed off to Assisi, with a female companion, three spiritual daughters, and more than a hundred other people from Urbino and Cagli, with enough money for eight days.[11] And they paused in Gubbio, where they abandoned so many supplies that a hundred others feasted on them. There was a certain gentleman of Gubbio who was sick. The doctors who had treated him had given up on him. Having heard of the servant of God's reputation, he asked that she come to visit him, out of charity and love of God. And convinced by his prayers and the prayers of others on his behalf, she went to visit him. And touching him with her holy hands and urging him to have patience, suddenly his customary and original health was, in fact, restored to him.[12] And a whole crowd of people who were then present saw this, including a spiritual woman from Urbino named Lady Jacoma, along with Lady Agnes, her companion. And many others were there and who should not be passed over in silence.[13] Then she returned to her inn, and all night she beat herself with slaps and blows, crying the whole time out of fervent charity. When such a miracle became publicly known, the next morning at daybreak the people ran to her. She was disturbed by this, and going out in public, she said: "Here is the dishonest and gluttonous woman. Here is the public sinner!" Thus she left the group. And a little later, the women returned and found her under a tree. And since it was raining hard at that moment, they marveled greatly at the blows of the night before, which had greatly weakened her, and at the other martyrdoms and misfortunes she had had endured, and at the rain.

50. With her reassembled companions, she left and arrived at a place called Baroncello, where, once she had entered the inn, there was a blind young boy whom she did not know.[14] Caressing him, as was her habit to do with everyone, she called him to her. While caressing him, she touched him, putting her hand on his head. And with these caresses, of the sort women are sweetly accustomed to give, the long-lost light was returned to him with the favor of the highest Creator. This happened so that she would be more fervent in prayer and so that her more merciful works would be better known, from which the saying of the Gospel could be said, *Virtue went out from her and cured all*.[15]

51. In the morning, at daybreak, she set out on the road with the female companions and finally arrived at Assisi. There, many spiritual women visited her and spoke to her, with great consolation for all, speaking and conferring about the worthy and holy work of Almighty God. When the time of the indulgence arrived,[16] she called her female companions the day before [the indulgence], and sweetly admonished them, saying: "My beloved little sisters (*sorelle*), leave behind the pleasures of this life and chase far away from you the clouds and errors of sin! Love virtues, and raise your spirit to the highest joys of God![17] Offer your humble prayers to heaven! As is said and sung in the Mass, *Sursum corda*,[18] Lift up your heart to the heights, so that God may make you worthy and deserving of such an indulgence!" In the morning, before daybreak, she left with the female companions to go to Santa Maria degli Angeli.[19] And when they were leaving the territory and the gate of Assisi[20]—marvelous to say!—she was carried off, and there was not one of her female companions, no matter how fast she could walk, who could catch up to her or touch her, and she was continuously carried this way in front of their eyes.[21] Having arrived at the church square of the place, Sister Clare was rapt and remained in ecstasy, seemingly for several hours. And having returned and been recalled to her original state, she began to cry grievously and to bathe her cheeks with many tears. Thus God gave her such grace that she saw and knew that all her company and herself deserved to have acquired the said indulgence. And thus she and all [her female companions] returned happily to Rimini.

52. When she had returned, and having at Venice a spiritual daughter whom she greatly loved, out of ardor for her she decided to go see her because it had been a long time since she had seen her. And suddenly, as if it had been diligently done by a public announcement, many people hurried to the house in which she was; and from noon until evening, they spoke with one another, coming and going like ants.

53. Her fertile speech was of such power that gamblers, gluttons, and those given to dishonesty all totally abstained [from these activities]. Women who were lascivious and hardened in countless wicked deeds, thanks to her correction, lived honestly and with virtue from then on. Among them, three grand and very rich noble ladies, blackened by very public wickedness, were converted by her kind and determined conversations; and putting aside their ornaments and necklaces, they dressed in beige and wore a cilice. And then they were praised for the goodness of their works and the clarity of their reputation. They did not return from it to their original lasciviousness, preserving a most praiseworthy life so that they might repose in the Lord and arrive at their final day.[22]

54. In those days, highly educated men who had mastered sacred mysteries and divine writings, as well as other highly virtuous men better than the others, having heard of her fame and seeing her visited by all the people and other foreigners, came to her; and each one posed a question to her concerning the writings of the saints and divine theology.[23] Then the Lord inspired her, and with the help of the Holy Spirit, she resolved these questions so well and with such clarity that she satisfied them wonderfully.[24] And after having left her, they all truly affirmed: "*The Holy Spirit is in* her[25] and speaks through her and guides her."[26]

55. Among other things, [she received] such grace that, for a long time, she knew the fates of herself and of others. She warned to be on guard against them, especially certain of her sisters and female friends, frequently predicting: "Train yourself to be steadfast and strong, because just as one who battles may hope for glory, so those who do not fight will not gain the palm,[27] unless you will be *proved as gold in the furnace*.[28] As it is said: Soon, you will suffer tribulations.[29] Be vigilant,

for the *lion that roars* is always searching for whom he may *devour*,[30] like *the thief* who comes *in the night*."[31] And she did not cease to predict such things, except so that vainglory would not trouble her, or so that certain people would not publicly call her a soothsayer.[32]

*   *   *

Our hagiographer has already dedicated Chapter 7 to Clare's success in converting others. Now, after detailing the foundation of her community (Chapters 8 and 9), in Chapter 10 he further develops his picture of Clare as a modern apostle but with a new degree of mobility. Indeed, he revisits several of the same stories first evoked in Chapter 7, spinning them out in greater detail. It may be that our author was not quite sure when these events had happened; he may also have wanted to stress the continuity of this theme throughout Clare's career. In any case, these episodes tend to replicate a now-familiar story line: initial obstacles are overcome at the price of new accusations, which are finally resolved through proof of divine approval.

"A certain poor little woman came to Sister Clare." It sounds like the beginning of a fairy tale. The phrase *poverella donna* ("poor little woman"), however, returns us to the vocabulary around Franciscan poverty. St. Francis was often called the *Poverello*, and he himself referred to Clare of Assisi and her sisters at San Damiano as *poverelle*. This impoverished woman's problem was that her daughter did not have the funds necessary to enter the *religione* of the Santuccia sisters, a community that had been founded by 1270, just outside the walls of Rimini, near the gate of Sant'Andrea (see Map 2, in Chapter 5). It housed sisters who followed the way of life established by Santuccia Carabotti of Gubbio (c. 1240–1305). The Santuccia sisters followed a modified version of the Benedictine Rule but devoted themselves to works of charity, gathering alms to help others. Their origins were thus not dissimilar to those of Clare's emerging foundation. But by the time of their founder's death, in March 1305, the Santuccia sisters were adhering to a strict social hierarchy typical of many established female orders. In most Benedictine convents, the choir nuns came from aristocratic backgrounds, while "lay sisters" were of humbler extraction. The Order of St. Clare drew many of its nuns from the urban patrician (like Clare of Rimini's family) or merchant class, but also accepted serving sisters (still real members of the community) from a lower social stratum. Other women might become tertiaries or, in northern Europe, beguines. Clare of Rimini's own community is one of the best-documented examples of an experiment in blurring these social distinctions.

The issue was the dowry. Starting in the twelfth century, it became increasingly common for a nobleman to give property or rents to his new son-in-law at the time of his daughter's marriage. The practice extended to young women who became nuns, or "brides of Christ." In other words, a substantial entrance fee was usually necessary for a woman to enter a traditional nunnery. Of course, some women whose families could easily afford such a fee nevertheless preferred a path of evangelical poverty. Douceline of Digne (d. 1274), for instance, could have become a nun of the Order of St. Clare at Genoa but chose to found the first two houses of beguines in Provence; similarly, Margherita Colonna's family of Roman aristocrats had arranged her entrance to Santa Chiara in Assisi, but she preferred an active life engaged with the poor. At the time of her conversion, could Clare of Rimini have afforded the entrance fee to a house like the Santuccia sisters? Perhaps not, in light of her family's exile and ill fortune. In any case, now Clare rose to "correct and amend the greed" of the local Santuccia sisters by positioning herself as the incarnation of apostolic poverty and reminding them of Christ's own charity. Her effective rhetorical strategy was to quote the parable of the rich young man (Matt. 19:21, 29). Jesus tells the young man, "If you will be perfect, go sell what you have and give to the poor and you shall have treasure in heaven, and come follow me," and then promises the apostles that "everyone that has left house, or brothers, or sisters, or father, or mother, or wife, or children, or lands, for my name's sake, shall receive a hundredfold reward, and shall possess life everlasting."

Santuccia Carabotti had set out on a path not so different from Clare's, not so long ago. She, too, had been married, and had separated from her husband by mutual consent. She built a new religious house near Gubbio, calling her sisters "servants" of Mary. Success led to new foundations, and soon Santuccia was the abbess of a network of more than twenty convents, granted papal protection by Clement IV (r. 1265–1268). At Rimini, these sisters were still called "mendicants" in 1299, but this label no longer reflected social reality. Clare's invocation of the Gospel message reminds them of their original vocation, shaming them into living up to their own ideals.

The succeeding miraculous anecdote serves to prove Clare's powers of intercession: a peasant woman (*una donna contadina*) is suffering from breast cancer, and the Santuccia abbess and sisters turn to Clare. Sure enough, at Clare's touch, the swelling in the breast subsides. Amid the rejoicing, Clare credits the cure to "the most kind Creator" and returns "to her cell." Clare, with her message of evangelical poverty and perfection, capped off with a miraculous healing, positions herself as a force for spiritual renewal, combating the hierarchical complacency into which (according to our hagiographer) the Santuccia sisters have fallen.

The third paragraph of Chapter 10 suddenly changes scene. "At this time," Clare encountered a "vain" and "pompous" widow. The reader has a sudden feeling of déjà vu, since the story of this "certain noble countess" has already been told more briefly in Chapter 7. What were her faults? She dressed in a sumptuous manner unbefitting a woman who has lost her husband, instead going out riding and hunting with her brother, wearing "a silver belt at her waist," adorned with multicolored squirrel fur, and galloping through valleys and over mountains, as though widowhood were a freedom to be enjoyed. Indeed, our hagiographer repeatedly stresses her excessively close relationship with her brother, as if to suggest some impropriety. How did this countess, at the pinnacle of the social pyramid, come to Clare's attention? Another "sister," also named Clare, spoke to our heroine and urged her to visit and correct this widow. Sensing an opportunity, Clare somehow scrapes an acquaintance with the countess, and "after a little while," innocently asks why she does not remarry, since it would remove all suspicion from her frivolous actions. The countess replies that she has not found a pleasing potential spouse. Clare has her rejoinder ready: "Then take eternal God, who is more noble than you, and of more generous parentage and family, who neither grows old nor becomes deformed or ugly over time, who will reign forever and ever!" Clare's words strike home, and the tearful countess falls into her arms, declaring her intention to follow this exhortation. A few days later, Clare cuts the countess's hair, signaling her departure from the secular world. According to the first version of the story (in Chapter 7), the countess "was received in a religious manner among the number of her sisters" and adopted "the habit and religion of the servant of Christ." And ever after (how else to end a fairy tale?), this reformed countess lived piously, as did her brother and all her family.

If the story feels familiar, it is not only because the hagiographer tells it twice. It is also an obvious echo of Clare's own conversion. This countess is from a higher social class, yet the sequence is the same: a well-born married woman leaves behind the vanities of the world and seeks Christ as her spouse, turning to a life of penance without (apparently) taking the formal vows of a nun. It is not the smoothest narrative in the text; the hagiographer ties himself in knots trying to clarify the roles of the two "Clares" in the tale (in the process, labeling Clare of Rimini as *beata* for the final time). Still, the episode in this longer telling has a sly logic, as Clare insinuates herself into the countess's circle, bides her time, eschews a frontal attack until just the right psychological moment, and then pounces like a cat on its prey. Clare's argument echoes the words that the Virgin Mary had spoken to her, years ago, in the church of St. Francis: What good is an earthly husband, no matter how rich or noble, who will age and sicken and die, when instead you could choose the Eternal Spouse, Christ?

As always, however, Clare oversteps the obvious bounds of her authority. By what right or rite does she cut the countess's hair to signal her entry into a religious way of life? Francis and his brothers had performed a similar ritual on the young Clare of Assisi when she ran away from home to join their "brotherhood." Margherita Colonna had cut her own hair, in a hymn-singing ritual that she seems to have invented herself, and dressed herself in a hair shirt covered with cheap cloth, imitating the sisters of the Order of St. Clare. But our Clare assumes the role of Francis or a cleric, by investing the repentant countess herself with the signs of a penitent.

The third episode in the chapter (after the affair of the Santuccia sisters and conversion of the widowed countess) is a new example, short but dramatic, of Clare's penchant for public drama. A "certain poor woman" frantically begs for money to pay a fine that the Commune of Rimini has levied against her husband. Clare most often intervenes on behalf of women; either they are poor and in need of help, or rich and in need of reform. In this case, the problem is again a lack of money. If the poor woman's husband cannot pay the fine, he will be sentenced to lose his hand. Probably, the judgment was for falsifying a document or bearing false witness, since the Rimini communal statutes specified this mutilation as the punishment for those crimes. The man would have been sentenced by the Commune's tribunal and given a limited time to pay his fine, or face losing a hand. Unfortunately, he was too poor to avoid mutilation—hence his wife's desperate attempts to raise the necessary sum by begging. It is the wife who draws Clare's pity. Clare hurries to the town square, next to the city hall, where there is a stone on which the auctioneer stands for public auctions. There she puts herself up for sale, no more and no less: she asks passersby "to buy her, to buy back a hand" (*la volesse comprare, per recomprare uno mano*).

Suddenly, the "Malatesta lords," rulers of the city, enter the narrative. Having "heard about what such a little woman (*donnicella*) had done," they summon Clare, grant her mercy, and allow the husband to go free. The reference to plural "Malatesta lords" tell us that this episode occurred between 1317 and 1326, when Ferrantino Malatesta shared power with his uncle Pandolfo. As the real lords of the city, the Malatesta could exercise the power of clemency, even while allowing the communal courts to handle day-to-day justice. In its judicial precision, this entire story is a powerful confirmation of the *Life*'s legal and social exactitude. Against this realistic background, the striking element is the power of a *donnicella* to sway the powerful Malatesta. The label is again analogous to the male *fraticello*, a diminutive label that could have a dismissive or endearing resonance, depending on context. A decade or two after Clare had ceased her Good Friday rituals, here she is again, in public, crying for attention in a bid to sway hearts and minds. Not even the Malatesta can resist. Did they realize that their progenitor, the "old mastiff," had persecuted Clare's father and brother, leading to their executions? Again, it is as though Clare's own story appears in reverse; as a young woman, she could not save her father's head or her brother's; now, as a religious figure with a public reputation, a *donnicella* but the leader of a burgeoning community of penitents, she saves a hand.

The chapter arrives at its real thrust as Clare takes to the road as a pilgrim and apostle: "At this time" (which should suggest 1317–1326), "Sister Clare headed off to Assisi." The statement is matter-of-fact, as though there were nothing unusual in a woman "with a female companion" and "three spiritual daughters" hitting the road for a 170-kilometer walk to Assisi. It would have taken two days to walk the sixty kilometers (thirty-seven miles) to Urbino, and another day to cover the remaining thirty-five to Cagli. Clare already knew Urbino (where she had been exiled) and must have had contacts in Cagli, too (remember that we have met Sister Benedetta of Cagli). As she passed through these towns, her following must have swollen, since by the fourth day, her group had grown to "more than a hundred." The next stop was Gubbio, in Umbria, another thirty kilometers (nineteen miles) down the road (we will meet Sister Viola of Gubbio). There the caravan paused to hand out its apparently overflowing supplies (see Map 1, in Chapter 1).

In Gubbio, Clare was summoned by a "certain gentleman" (*certo gintilhomo*) who was so ill that his doctors had given up treating him. Evidently, Clare's reputation preceded her. Of course, the man was healed, in front of a whole crowd of witnesses, including Clare's "companion," now named as Lady Agnes, and Lady Jacoma, "a spiritual woman from Urbino," who probably joined Clare's entourage during the trip. Clare reacts to divine favor as she always does, with self-recrimination and self-flagellation; she returns to her inn to "beat herself with slaps and blows." As crowds gather the next morning, Clare publicly calls herself a dishonest, gluttonous sinner (just as Francis had done before her), and runs to hide under a tree in the pouring rain. When her companions find her, they marvel at the way she sits suffering from her self-inflicted blows, pelted by the raindrops. It would have been so easy for our hagiographer to add the expected flourish by saying that Clare remained miraculously dry! He resists the temptation, giving us instead a vivid image of Clare miserable in her wet clothes.

The next stop was Baroncello, only ten kilometers (six miles) farther on toward Assisi. The caravan's progress had evidently been slowed down by the episode at Gubbio, though it is also true that climbing the road through the Apennines would not have been easy. Here, on the last night before reaching Assisi, Clare cures a blind boy at the inn. In both cures, Clare heals with her hands, but in this instance, the hagiographer emphasizes (three times) that she "caressed" the boy, "as women are sweetly accustomed" to do. He seems almost wistful, perhaps remembering the touch of his own mother, or dreaming just for a moment of the feminine contacts that his vows oblige him to avoid.

At last, they began the final thirty-five kilometers (twenty-two miles) to Assisi. In a certain sense, Clare's life had been pointing toward the city of St. Francis and St. Clare for decades. Within Assisi's newly expanded walls, on the eastern edge of town, were the twelfth-century cathedral of San Rufino in the aristocratic neighborhood where St. Clare's family had lived; and, a little south, the new basilica of St. Clare (Santa Chiara) built between 1257 and 1265 on the site of the earlier San Giorgio. On the western edge of Assisi was the sprawling, multileveled basilica of St. Francis (San Francesco), begun just before his canonization in 1228. But the original sites of Franciscan memory lay outside the city. Leaving through the *porta nuova* (new gate) near Santa Chiara and descending a hillside filled with olive trees, pilgrims could reach the tiny sanctuary of San Damiano. There, Francis had experienced a formative moment in his conversion, in 1206, and had rebuilt the dilapidated stone church with his own hands. In 1211 or 1212, Clare of Assisi and her first companions settled there, living in proudly precarious poverty.

Farther down into the valley was the Portiuncula, also known as Santa Maria degli Angeli, a crude little church restored by Francis in 1208. Here, Francis had first grasped his calling to preach the Gospel like a new apostle. From 1210 on, Francis and his small band of followers were based at the Portiuncula; St. Clare joined the brothers there briefly (this is where her hair was cut, in a sign of her religious vocation) before moving to San Damiano. The annual general chapters of the growing order met there, and it was there that Francis died during the night of October 3–4, 1226. Today, the little church is encased in a colossal dome; but in the early fourteenth century, it was still a humble chapel in the open air, a sacred spot full of Franciscan history and memory.

Although pilgrims might come at any time, certain dates drew them like magnets. St. Clare's feast day was fixed to August 12 but never truly gripped the public imagination. Francis's feasts were far more popular. His main feast, the day of his death (or, for a saint, his birth into his true, heavenly life), was October 4. But there was also the feast of his translation (the date on which his body had been moved to the new basilica) on May 25, and, on September 17, the commemoration of his reception of the stigmata (not formalized by the papacy until 1340 but popularly celebrated much earlier). Finally, there was the tradition of the "Portiuncula Indulgence" (also known as the "Pardon" or "Forgiveness of Assisi"). Later witnesses insisted that Pope Honorius III had granted Francis's request that anyone visiting the little chapel would receive remission of all punishment for their sins. Whatever the historical reality of this claim, by Clare of Rimini's time, the pilgrimage to the Portiuncula was particularly popular within Spiritual Franciscan circles and centered on August 1 and 2.

This indulgence was the goal of Clare's journey to Assisi. Her troupe must have left Rimini in late July. After six days on the road, they arrive at Assisi, where they intend to pray and wash away their sins. Evidently, they have several days to wait, time enough for "many spiritual women" to speak with Clare, "with great consolation for all." On the eve of the indulgence (probably August 1), Clare gathers her companions for what can only be called a sermon. She urges her beloved "little sisters" (*sorelle*) to leave behind the sins of the world and to embrace virtue. She cites the Psalms in her exhortation to "raise your spirits to the highest joys of God!" And then, in a final stroke of daring, she cries, "as is said in the Mass, *Sursum corda*, Lift up your heart to the heights!" *Sursum corda*—these are the only two words in Latin in the entire *Life*. In reciting them, Clare boldly reproduces, for a brief moment, the effect of a priest intoning the preface of the Eucharistic prayer, around the middle of the Mass, between offertory and consecration.

A gray area might exist between a pious matron's acceptable exhortation in private, on the one hand, and a woman's unacceptable public preaching, on the other; but Clare's move to mimic the words of a priest performing Mass ran every risk of catapulting her squarely into a new condemnation. Her "female companions" may have basked in her spiritual glow at the time, and our hagiographer is always willing to put Clare's most controversial actions before the reader's eyes. But what would clerics in Assisi have thought? How would a less enthusiastic churchman have reacted if he read this *Life* years later? Clare was not even an abbess or a senior nun teaching her sisters but merely an unlearned laywoman, in a foreign city, fearless in her effrontery.

The next morning (presumably, August 2) before dawn, Clare and her companions descend from Assisi to the Portiuncula. But while the others pick their way down the hill, Clare is "carried off." By angels (as in Chapter 8)? By miraculous levitation? Our author does not say; but apparently, Clare seems to float down the slope, far ahead. Arriving at the church, she is rapt into ecstasy for hours, dissolving into tears when this state comes to an end. Our hagiographer has no access to her experience on this level; he tells us only that Clare knows that she and all her companions have achieved what they sought: they "deserved to have acquired the said indulgence." By this simple revelation, we are again assured that God has approved of Clare's actions, however much they may shock onlookers. In this spotless state, Clare's band "returned happily to Rimini."

This road trip must have been deeply satisfying, for Clare seems to have developed a sudden fondness for travel. "When she had returned" to Rimini, she decided to depart once again—this time, for Venice. So far as we know, Assisi was as far south as she ever voyaged, and Venice as far north. Medieval women did occasionally make lengthy pilgrimages—for instance, to Jerusalem or Santiago de Compostela. Clare's horizons, by contrast, were limited to the less than 300 kilometers (185 miles) between Assisi and Venice. What is striking is the sense that across this still rather considerable stretch of road, Clare somehow managed to build up a real network of spiritual friends. In this case, she traveled to Venice to see "a spiritual daughter whom she greatly loved" but whom she had not seen for "a long time." Does this mean that Clare had been to Venice before? More likely, this "daughter" was from the region of Rimini and had at some point moved to the Veneto, farther up the Adriatic coast. But we have seen evidence of Clare's connections in Urbino, Cagli, Gubbio, Mercatello, and now in Venice, where, upon her arrival "many people hurried to the house in which she was," as though her presence had been made known "by a public announcement." Indeed, in one of our hagiographer's more vivid images, these people scurried about, coming and going "like ants" in their eagerness to speak with the visiting penitent.

But were ants useful animals or harmful pests? Clare's life and *Life* give us a series of glimpses into the informal world of unenclosed religious women; groups that would have been called beguines in the north and that in Italy were known by various titles such as *bizzoche*. Such groups had flourished during the thirteenth century; but from the time of the Second Council of Lyon, in 1274, churchmen had grown more and more suspicious of them. Indeed, the decade following 1317—when Clare's road trips seem to have occurred—saw the church subjecting beguines to deep suspicion and sustained scrutiny. Following the Council of Vienne in 1311–1312, Clement V issued a scathing indictment of "women commonly known as beguines," who "promise obedience to nobody, nor renounce possessions, nor profess any approved rule." If the pope was fulminating largely against the beguines of the Rhineland and Low Countries, the suspicion was generalized by the time the "Clementine" decrees were formally issued by John XXII in 1317. Indeed, in 1326, John specifically warned the bishops of Lombardy and Tuscany to be on guard against such women without a real rule or canonical religious habit, who dared to dispute and preach on the mysteries of the faith—the very portrait of Clare!

For, as the last three episodes of Chapter 10 illustrate, Clare continued to preach, teach, and even prophesy. First, another story is repeated and amplified from Chapter 7, in which Clare's "fertile speech" converts "three grand and very rich noble ladies, blackened by very public wickedness." Their rather generic sins evidently concern "lasciviousness," from which they are turned by Clare's "conversations." Then we find another example of Clare's penchant for debating with learned men. "In those days, highly educated men," apparently university-educated masters of the sacred page, sought her out and tested her with questions "concerning the writings of the saints and divine theology." Inspired by the Lord, Clare "resolved these questions" with such clarity (*chiaramente*, the old pun: "in such Clare-like fashion") that they all agreed that the Holy Spirit spoke through her. In truth, the scene is even more dramatic than previous moments (such as with the tyrant Bolognino) in which Clare had converted learned men. In this instance, these were true professionals, masters of theology, challenging Clare to the standard university exercise of a *quaestio disputata* (a disputed theological question). In this staple of scholastic practice, a difficult issue would be posed for a master's consideration; he would weigh evidence for both sides, give his favored resolution, and then explain why the opposing arguments could not hold up.

Medieval holy women did interact with university men. For instance, the lector (university-educated teacher) for the Franciscan convent in Paris once approached Douceline of Digne in Marseille to ask: "Lady Douceline, what is the soul?" She first humbly demurred, but then entered a rapturous state and answered (in Latin): "What is the soul? The mirror of divine majesty!" The "great lector" was forced to agree that "all the masters and teachers in Paris could not have given a better solution to the question." Other beguines engaged, directly or at a distance, with such university-inspired disputes in their writings—just the sort of behavior that had raised the church's ire. Most famously, the beguine Marguerite Porete communicated with the famous master of theology Godfrey of Fontaines and flirted with formulations akin to disputed questions in her French *Mirror of Simple Souls*. But Marguerite was burned alive as a relapsed heretic in Paris in 1310.

Indeed, the most powerful means open to medieval women who wished to speak on controversial issues was to present themselves as mouthpieces of God, claiming to reveal his prophetic words rather than speak their own. Thus our hagiographer is careful to have the learned masters declare: "The Holy Spirit is in her and speaks through her and guides her!" The last episode in the chapter immediately softens Clare's intellectual effrontery with a related move into the prophetic realm. Clare received—from God, we should understand—the grace of knowing the fates of her sisters and friends. She, like Francis and other holy figures, could predict who would find glory and who would face tribulation. Still, and again, our hagiographer walks a tightrope; he cannot allow himself to fall off on the side of Clare's overly confident knowledge-claims, but neither can he topple over into suggesting access to any kind of forbidden knowledge. Clare, he quickly adds, only let up on these predictions so that "certain people" would not call her a soothsayer, an *indivinatrice*, in the medieval Italian (from the Latin *divinatrix*; modern Italian is *divinatrice*). Clare had been labeled a patarine and chased through the streets years earlier; the last thing she needed now was to be called a sorceress. Again, the danger was real. In the same years that Marguerite Porete was imprisoned and burned in Paris, a woman named Margueronne of Bellevillette had been accused of using her powers as a *divinatrix* to abet a plot to murder the queen of France. Margueronne was clapped into prison, just a few hundred meters from where Marguerite met her end, and remained there for at least a decade.

*　　*　　*

Scholars have long argued over the place of women in medieval society. Some have seen them as victims of patriarchy and misogyny, and some as powerful actors in their own lives. Clare's *Life* offers its own response, for whatever it may be worth. Nothing is a simple binary, and everything is embedded into the many layers that make up medieval culture. Clare's life, by this time, has been both a decades-long renunciation and a constant battle with political power, churchmen, and learned men. In this chapter, we have seen successive fights between poor and rich, humble and powerful, simple and educated, women and men. Clare is a master at finding ideological cracks through which she can enter these contests, forcing open her own space and forging her own path. She never ceases her renunciations and never stops asserting her own will. She has the courage of her convictions, and she triumphs in her encounters with nobles, with the Malatesta lords, and with university masters. But each triumph necessitates a fresh renunciation and a new wave of penance. Even her victories are dangerous; every success comes at a price.

CHAPTER 11

The Power of Images

56. Sister Clare had a special vision, when it seemed to her she had in her heart an entire little boy, as appears above on folio eight.[1] Another time, it seemed to Sister Clare that she was building a bridge, across which many different people would have to pass. Other times, it seemed to her that she was digging under the earth with her head, and entered it the way a plow does. And it was necessary to dig a big ditch, which would be an ample burial place for her; and her chest was so seriously oppressed that the breath could not escape from any part of her body.

57. She seemed further to see in spirit that the female companions ordered (*ordinassero*) themselves against her and strove to persecute her. And so immediately, she called to them and said to them, "Have you ever heard any quarrel from me, or that I have spoken badly of you?" They answered, "No, dearest mother." And she [replied], "Think well about this, and tell me the truth, in clarity." And they replied similarly, "Believe, mother, and accept it for certain, that we will never deviate from your order (*vostro ordine*),[2] nor will we be contrary to your will (*tua voluntà*),[3] until we reach our final day! Speak, command, and we will obey!" And thus all her distasteful harassment ceased.

58. One time, she had risen for the divine office and to examine her faults, before midnight, with penitence, tears, and howls, as was her custom. When she had suffered many martyrdoms, she paused as though exhausted; a sound came to her ears that said, "Sit, and do not open your eyes, because of the splendor!" And then, in spirit, there

appeared to her a throne of wonderful size and unaccustomed gran-
deur, most beautiful and splendid in every ornament, above which sat
the Master of masters, surrounded by the apostolic order along with
John the Baptist. And when she saw herself made glorious by the reception of such a family, then he showed her his wounded right side;
because of this showing, she more ardently asked for what she wanted.
And seeing this, she asked insistently for mercy, and prayed with a
great abundance of tears, recommending herself and her female companions, with her benefactors and spiritual daughters, whom she
named this way with fervor and with all her heart. And then, the said
Master gave St. John a book with letters written in gold, and said to
him, "Give it to her!" And she kissed it, on her knees. The Lord said,
"*My peace I give to you,* my *peace I leave with you.*"[4] And he disappeared. And she remained consoled with all sweetness. These things
happened three days before the feast of St. Leonard,[5] and her Sisters
Amata, Agnes, and Agnesina, standing at the doorway, heard many
words. And thus from then on, Sister Clare was of more evident virtue than before to her sisters and others.[6]

*   *   *

The short Chapter 11 is among the most intricately revealing sections of
the *Life.* Its basic structure should come as no surprise to anyone who has
followed our hagiographer's favorite strategies to this point: the first and third
paragraphs describe powerful visions, in order to contain and diffuse an
anxiety-producing crisis related in the second.

Visions authenticate revelations in many literary genres, including the sacred texts of the major monotheistic traditions. They appear frequently in
the Torah, the New Testament, and the Qur'an, often as the starting point
for the interpretation of the divine message. Many saints' lives are equally
filled with visions; the two *Lives* of Margherita Colonna, for example, might
almost be described as a series of visions strung together with connecting
text. How should we treat the record of such experiences? Most modern readers will be inclined to doubt their veracity. Should we simply dismiss them
as infantile delusions produced by a credulous age? Or treat them as purely
rhetorical constructs? It may be more useful to place the visionary's interior

voyage alongside the hagiographer's intentions, in order to more fully appreciate the intersection of their two perspectives.

Beginning with Clare of Rimini's dramatic experience in the Franciscan church of Rimini (Chapter 2), we have repeatedly seen how her visionary imagination shapes her spiritual expression. In Chapter 11, our hagiographer begins with a nod to this continuity by referring back to Clare's "special vision," in which a little child clung to her heart, which he has already mentioned (Chapter 5). The second visionary image related here is new in our text but not strikingly novel: it "seemed" to Clare that "she was building a bridge, across which many different people (*molte persone et gente*) would have to pass." Thus Clare imagines herself as a sort of conduit, leading others to salvation. This vision might seem vain (Clare presenting herself as a savior), but it is also a sign of humility, since a bridge is necessarily trampled by the people who cross it.

The third vision in this first paragraph is startlingly original. Clare sees herself "digging under the earth with her head," and she "entered it the way a plow does." Suddenly, this plowing of the earth is revealed to be Clare's own grave, and in her dreamlike panic, "her chest was so seriously oppressed that the breath could not escape from any part of her body." The sequence of images is terrifyingly precise. What saint had ever imagined using her head as a shovel to dig her own grave? Whatever spiritual or allegorical interpretation the medieval or modern reader might apply, the raw power of this imagery underscores Clare's visual imagination and her hagiographer's visceral flair for rendering it verbally. Perhaps this unusual image draws on the parable of the sower (Matt. 13:1–23; Mark 4:1–20; Luke 8:4–15), in which Jesus tells of a farmer whose indiscriminately scattered seeds grow only when they encounter good soil. It may also allude to Jesus's words in John 12:24–25: "Amen, amen, I say to you, unless the grain of wheat falling into the ground dies, it remains alone. But if it dies it brings forth much fruit. Whoever loves their life shall lose it, and whoever hates their life shall keep it unto eternal life." The anguished image might thus contain a hopeful message: Clare is the good soil from which the divine word may sprout and the kernel that must die in order to reach eternal life.

The hagiographer begins the second paragraph as though intending to continue the visionary theme: "She seemed further to see in spirit. . . ." Saints were often understood to be able to see what people tried to keep hidden in their minds. Our hagiographer has already attributed a similar power to Clare in Chapter 10. Here, however, this gift of clairvoyance allows Clare to perceive the very real fact that her "female companions ordered themselves against her and strove to persecute her." What was the nature of this simmering rebellion, in which Clare's sisters draw themselves up in order against her (*contra lei ordinassero*), but eventually relent and promise never again to deviate from her order (*dal vostro ordine mai non ce disviarimo*)? These women had chosen Clare freely as their model and mother. They fervently admired her uncompromising life of penance. But how was their life to be "ordered" on a mundane, day-to-day level? As we have seen, the sisters followed no canonical rule and, indeed, made up no religious order in the formal sense. They had only a vague approval from a passing cardinal and nothing but the words and example of their charismatic founder as a practical guide. Some of these sisters seem to have adopted a mode of life that Clare saw as opposed to the "order" that she sought to impose. Questioned and confronted ("Have you ever heard any quarrel from me, or that I have spoken badly of you?"), the sisters quickly relent, addressing Clare as "dearest mother" and promising not only to adhere to "your order" (*vostro ordine*) but "to your will" (*a la tua voluntà*). The two are really one: Clare embodies her own order, and her wishes are the closest thing to a rule. Indeed, the Italian contains a telling difference between the two uses of "your," which is not directly translatable into English. *Vostro* is the formal address, suitable for a respected lawgiver; *tua* is familiar, acknowledging the wishes of a beloved mother. Clare is both at once, incarnating authority and care. Such a powerful and charismatic combination seems irresistible, until the moment when it becomes too much to bear.

Many founders of religious orders, even the most successful, experienced moments like this. At the Dominican general chapter meeting in 1220, St. Dominic himself offered to resign his position of leadership, following a rejection of his proposal to assign administrative roles to illiterate converts within the order. At exactly the same moment, in 1220, St. Francis resigned as minister general of his own order, fuming about how the *Fratres Minores* had lost their way. Again, the climax came at a general chapter meeting, where Francis accused his brothers of betraying his own example: "And the Lord told me what he wanted: he wanted me to be a new fool in the world! God did not wish to lead us by any other path than by this knowledge, but God will confound you by your knowledge and wisdom!" (sarcasm drips from the phrase "knowledge and wisdom"). The shift from "me" to "you," from Francis's sense of divine mission to his prophetic threats against his own followers, marks the anguished realization that even the founder's charisma has its limits. Clare's crisis is slightly less dramatic. There is no formal chapter meeting to provide a charged setting. But the dynamic is the same. The sisters raise doubts: we have chosen to follow your example, but now we wonder whether we might not do better without your heavy-handed leadership. In the end, neither Francis nor Dominic was discarded or disowned, nor is Clare. Her sisters relent and promise to "obey" until "we reach our final day."

Our hagiographer is a wonderful guide. He hides nothing in Clare's story. He reports the accusations of heresy, the dilemma over buying property, and even the opposition of her own companions. He merely tries to soften these blows, slipping them between ecstatic episodes to show that Clare's tribulations are only tests of her adherence to the divine will. Yet nothing blunts Clare's stubborn insistence that she always knows best (no matter how many times she has to punish herself to find reassurance). Read retrospectively, after the crisis of rebellion, her visions of the bridge and the plow seem to take on greater significance. Clare, in her own mind, is building a bridge for others, putting her hand to the plow on behalf of her sisters, dying like a grain of wheat planted so that it can burst forth anew. Even when facing a momentary betrayal (as though buried alive?), she cannot change course. Our hagiographer has provided several instances of Clare's sisters trying to soften her austerities. But Clare rarely seems to show this kind of softhearted compassion when dictating to others.

* * *

Our hagiographer, in order to wipe away the memory of insurrection, concludes the chapter with a further vision that Clare saw "in the spirit." But this time, the vision leads us down a labyrinthian path, where one image reflects another and inspires a third and a fourth. We need to retrace these steps carefully, one at a time.

The setting is just before midnight on November 3. We cannot be sure about the exact year, but we will see that it is probably no earlier than 1318. Clare has "risen for the divine office" but pauses, worn out by her customary

cries. She first hears a voice commanding her to sit and close her eyes. For-
tunately, those eyes are not necessary for her to see "the Master of masters"
atop a bishop's or university master's throne (*cathedra*, spelled *chathedra* in
the manuscript), surrounded by the apostles and John the Baptist. Jesus dis-
plays to Clare the wound in his side, and she begs him to show mercy to her
whole entourage (the very sisters who have just rebelled against her). Jesus
then hands St. John "a book with letters written in gold," telling him to give
it to Clare. She kneels and kisses the book, as Jesus quotes from John's own
Gospel (14:27): "My peace I give to you, my peace I leave with you" (*La mia
pace ve concedo, la pace mia ve lasso*). Then he vanishes. Sisters Amata, Agnes, and Agnesina, apparently listening from the doorway, hear some of the
words that were exchanged. Their presence demonstrates that the whole community perceives this dramatic vision as a vindication of Clare's leadership.
But since these sisters can hear only snatches of the conversation, it is up to
Clare to relate the details of what she has experienced.

We have seen that vivid visions are central to the spiritual expression of
holy women like Clare. Very often, however, the building blocks of such visions can be found in the pictorial environment that infuses these women's
daily lives. For instance, when Margherita Colonna had a vision of a preacher,
she identified him with Francis of Assisi because she was familiar with an
"image" or a "likeness" in which Francis was dressed in a similar manner (she
may have been referring to the famous early fresco of Francis at Subiaco). In
other words, a painting had first influenced Margherita's visionary imagination and then helped her to interpret the meaning of what she had seen.

In the case of Clare's vision, recent research has uncovered the source
of its iconographic underpinnings.[7] From at least 1069, the church that was
dedicated to St. John the Evangelist (San Giovanni) stood on the west side of
Rimini, near the Piazza del Comune, now known as the Piazza Cavour. In
1256, the bishop gave it to the Augustinian Hermits (the third mendicant order, after the Dominicans and the Franciscans); from then on, it was more
often known as Sant'Agostino. We recall that an earthquake struck Rimini
in 1308 (see the commentary to Chapter 9). Sant'Agostino suffered extensive
damage and had to be restored over the next decade. This collaborative project, necessitating a citywide effort, included a new program of frescoes, probably directed by the painters and brothers Giovanni, Giuliano, and Zangolo
of Rimini. The main part of the work may have been finished by 1318, when

the church welcomed the general chapter meeting of the Augustinian Hermits. But artistic fashions changed over the centuries, and Baroque stucco and chubby cherubs eventually covered up the fourteenth-century frescoes. The medieval artwork might have remained hidden forever, if not for another earthquake that struck Rimini on May 17, 1916. The stucco crumbled, the cherubs gave way, and the fourteenth-century frescoes once again came to light.

In recent decades, scholars have worked to reconstruct the iconographic program of the frescoes that originally covered the apse in the church of Sant'Agostino, considered among the most interesting examples of the Rimini school of painting, which flourished from the late thirteenth century into the early fifteenth. The faithful entering the church around 1318 would have encountered a huge representation of the Last Judgment painted into the triumphal arch atop the vaulted wall separating the choir of the Augustinians from the area open to the laity (see Figure 2; the fresco is partially reconstituted today in Rimini's Museo della Città). The imagery represents Christ as a judge with the sun and moon on either side and two rows of angels; those on the right brandish swords, and those on the left hold palms, a crown, and a trumpet. At the bottom, we see the apostles, the Virgin Mary, and probably (although the fresco is damaged here) St. John the Baptist.

The location of this representation was unusual; more often, the Last Judgment was represented on the interior wall of a church's facade, so that the faithful would see it as they left the sanctuary. But the church's original dedication to St. John explains this anomaly. Christians in medieval Europe traditionally regarded John the Evangelist (that is, the author of the book of John) as identical with John, the reputed author of the book of the Apocalypse (the final book of the New Testament, also known as the book of Revelation). Moreover, popular tradition, based on apocryphal texts such as the "Acts of John," filled out his story. According to these legends, during the persecution of the Emperor Domitian, John was brought from Ephesus to Rome, where he was immersed in a pot of boiling oil. He miraculously emerged unharmed, but was then imprisoned on the island of Patmos in the Aegean Sea, where he wrote the book of the Apocalypse. Upon his eventual return to Ephesus, he witnessed a terrible earthquake, and his preaching after a dispute with a pagan philosopher miraculously caused the collapse of a

Figure 2. Fresco representing the Last Judgment. Church of Sant'Agostino, Rimini, c. 1318. Museo della Città. Photograph by Gilberto Urbinati. Used by permission of the diocese of Rimini.

temple dedicated to the goddess Diana. Thus, one fresco in Sant'Agostino depicts John escaping unscathed from the boiling oil, and then seated in the act of writing with the pen in his right hand. Above him, angels with trumpets announce the vision of the Apocalypse that John is about to witness and translate in his writings. Another, with an implicit nod to Rimini's own recent experience, shows John contemplating the devastation of the earthquake in Ephesus (see Figure 3). The crumbling columns may refer to the destruction of Diana's temple.

In the background of the apse, we find the most striking representation: the risen Christ enthroned in glory, flanked by John the Baptist and John the Evangelist (see Figure 4). Jesus and the Evangelist each hold an open book, while the Baptist unfurls a scroll that reads: "Lamb of God, who removes the world's sin, have pity on us."

This image sums up the entire prophetic program, from one St. John to the other. The Baptist announces the coming of the Lamb of God, and hence the Passion and the Resurrection, while the prophet of Patmos announces the mysteries of the End, the return of Christ, and the Final Judgment.

Did Clare of Rimini meditate before these frescoes? Alas, we have no firm evidence that would place her at the church of San Giovanni/Sant'Agostino. But we know (our hagiographer has stressed it repeatedly) that she haunted the churches of Rimini. Clare could hardly have missed the exciting restoration of the church of the Augustinian Hermits as it progressed between 1308 and 1318. We know that popular themes of Christian art often imprinted

Figure 3. Fresco representing the story of the earthquake in Ephesus. Church of Sant'Agostino, Rimini, c. 1318. Museo della Città. Photograph by Gilberto Urbinati. Used by permission of the diocese of Rimini.

themselves on her mind, from her vision of the Virgin with heavenly host in the church of St. Francis, to her self-image crowned and carried by angels from the church of San Matteo, to the "little majesty" that led her to the house of Lapo. After Sant'Agostino reopened around 1318, Clare would almost certainly have come to gaze upon its glorious new frescoes.

Let's return to the content of her vision. What did Clare see that November 3? A wonderful *cathedra*, a bishop's or university master's throne. Two such thrones were depicted in the sanctuary of Sant'Agostino, one within the Last Judgment at the top of the triumphal arch, and the other as a throne of glory in the background of the apse. Then Clare saw the enthroned "Master of masters" surrounded by the apostles and John the Baptist. In Sant'Agostino, Jesus and the Baptist are again present in both places (arch and apse), while the apostles figure in the Last Judgment. Suddenly, the figures in Clare's vision seem to come alive. Christ shows Clare the wound in his side. The wound is not visible in the fresco of Christ enthroned but may have been in the Last Judgment (its current damaged state makes it difficult to be certain). At any rate, the wound is evoked in that painting by the angel brandishing a lance. As soon as Clare receives this privilege, Christ gives a book to John—surely the Evangelist. In Sant'Agostino, both Christ and John hold a book. Clare

Figure 4. Fresco representing Christ enthroned in glory with John the Baptist and John the Evangelist. Church of Sant'Agostino, Rimini, c. 1318. Museo della Città. Photograph by Gilberto Urbinati. Used by permission of the diocese of Rimini.

brings it to her lips for a kiss. Jesus at last speaks: "My peace I give to you, my peace I leave with you."

The vision begins with a wide-angle lens but becomes ever more focused on Christ and John the Evangelist. Clare's attention seems to move downward and back to front in Sant'Agostino, from the triumphant arch to the apse, where the Messiah is enthroned between the two Johns, with John the Baptist holding his scroll that refers to the "Lamb of God, who takes away the sins of the world." The passage comes from the book of John (1:29) but also makes up the liturgical invocation of the Agnus Dei in the Mass. To the first two times that the priest intones this line, the faithful respond, "Have pity on us"; to the third, "Give us peace." For any medieval Christian, the phrase would evoke the one that immediately precedes it in the liturgy: "Lord Jesus, you who said to your disciples, 'I give you my peace, I leave you my peace,' look not on our sins, but on the faith of your church." We can imagine Clare, focused intently on the Eucharistic rite in Sant'Agostino, latching on to these words while losing herself in the frescoes above and in front of her. She returns to her community, with her sisters. That night, or a night soon after, the scene sparks to life in her mind, seeming to swim before her very eyes. One circle is complete.

Another, however, is just beginning. Around 1330, a few years after Clare's death, a triptych was created in her memory, very likely at the instigation of the Franciscans of Rimini (see Figure 5). They must have commissioned a local painter (art historians have long debated his identity), who created a stunning triptych that was intended to decorate the altar in the modest sanctuary of Clare's surviving community. Today, it is preserved in the Musée Fesch in Ajaccio (Corsica, France).

The left-hand panel of the triptych represents the Adoration of the Magi. The central panel depicts the Crucifixion, with St. Francis at the feet of the emaciated Christ; the Virgin, the Magdalene, and two other women to the viewer's left; and St. John the Evangelist to the right. The right-hand panel is reserved for a scene from Clare's career. Read from left to right, the three panels sum up the life of Christ, from birth to death to resurrection, or from Nativity to Passion to Glory.

Which episode from Clare's life would be most effective to paint in the right-hand panel? Her most controversial moments were surely off-limits. The painter and his patrons thus elected to depict the vision of Clare with Christ and the two saints John. This gripping episode in the *Life of Clare* must have struck readers as particularly noteworthy, just as the hagiographer

Figure 5. Triptych depicting the Adoration of the Magi, the Crucifixion, and the Vision of Clare of Rimini, c. 1330 (attributed to Francesco of Rimini). Tempera and gold on wood, 51 × 147 cm. Used by permission of the Palais Fesch-Musée des Beaux-Arts d'Ajaccio.

intended. In the bottom-left corner of this panel, a small, kneeling Clare
(posthumously given a habit similar to that of a Franciscan tertiary) seems
about to kiss a book held out to her by John the Evangelist, on which is written
in golden letters (in Latin): "I give you my peace, I leave you my peace." Behind
John, a gigantic Christ offers his blessing, with a star-strewn robe pierced to
reveal the prominently displayed side wound. Behind him, John the Baptist
heads a gathering of haloed apostles and holds a scroll that reads: "Here is the
Lamb of God, you who takes away the sins of the world" (see Figure 6).

Figure 6. Vision of Clare of Rimini. Right panel of Figure 5. Used by permission
of the Palais Fesch-Musée des Beaux-Arts d'Ajaccio.

We can now follow the long and winding trail of words and images: biblical texts—the Apocalypse, the book of John, and apocryphal legends— inspire the program of frescoes in the renovated church of Sant'Agostino. These images, in turn, spark Clare's vision, which is written down by her hagiographer. Her *Life*, read and reread a few years later by her followers and admirers, inspires the painting of a triptych, which today provides us with our most vivid glimpse of Clare as she was remembered by those who had known her in the flesh.

Indeed, the scene was so important to Clare's community that a second triptych was made a decade or two later, which (at least later in its history)

Figure 7. Second version of the Vision of Clare of Rimini, c. 1335 (attributed to Francesco of Rimini). Tempera on wood, 55 × 60 cm. Used by permission of the National Gallery, London.

was displayed in the chapter hall of Santa Maria degli Angeli (the successor community to Clare's group in Rimini). Today, the left-hand panel (Adoration of the Magi) of this second version is in the Lowe Art Museum at the University of Miami, and the right-hand panel (Clare's vision) is in the National Gallery in London (see Figure 7). The central panel, which apparently featured not the Crucifixion but the Madonna and Child, is no longer known to exist. On the right, we again find the depiction of Clare's vision; this time, she is dressed in a checkered outfit that may recall the dress of some Franciscan-inspired penitents such as Margherita of Cortona. Moreover, the Baptist lacks his scroll. According to a recent reconstruction by Michela Messina, this triptych was then topped with a Crucifixion scene, which may be the one preserved in the Musée des Beaux-Arts in Strasbourg (France).

In both triptychs, Clare is the only figure without a halo. To the end, her admirers were careful about claiming saintly status for her. But even more powerfully than the *Life*, these paintings inscribe Clare in salvation history alongside the Virgin, St. Francis, and the heavenly choir of saints. Our hagiographer would probably have been pleased to know that his record of Clare's experience would eventually find such pictorial reinforcement.

Following our trail of images has led us past the point of Clare's death. Let us return to the *Life*, to see how our hagiographer brings his work to a close in Chapter 12.

CHAPTER 12

Through a Glass Darkly

59. At a certain time, God allowed that Sister Clare should be tempted by demons. And thus they harassed her so severely that there was no way she could sleep at night. And many times, they filled her cell, saying, "We will enter on top of you, and you will not be able to escape."[1] And she would answer, "If God permits this, it will not be without reason. I am worthy of it. May it be done according to the will of my Lord!"[2] When these words were said, [the demons] suddenly departed, ineffective. And because of the fear that Agnes and Amata felt, in order to rest more securely they slept in her cell. And when [Clare] was singing psalms, on her knees, on the beam on which she slept, [the demons] made her fall. And sometimes, during the day, they attacked her in such a strong fashion that, walking in the garden, she would call the female companions. And [the demons] caused her to have such a serious fall on a stone staircase that for a while, she limped and walked with a staff. And when she was in the garden, they made her fall to the ground with such damage that she lost a finger from her hand. And then God himself lifted all the demons' harassments from her. And so great and so many were her consolations and gifts without number, that it cannot be said with the tongue or written with a reed pen.

60. At this time, on the vigil of the Magdalene,[3] Sister Clare was raised up in such contemplation that she totally lost the power of speech. And when she returned to herself, she immediately entered her cell, and for five days in a row she remained always in contemplation, as two of her sisters, Amata and Viola of Gubbio, diligently noted.

61. Another time, at the conversion of St. Paul,[4] for a great number of days the servant of God abstained from drinking, because the
fast of Jesus, who had *fasted* in the desert *forty days and forty nights*,[5]
had returned to her memory. And then God's supreme virtue allowed
that his servant be afflicted by a great and unbearable thirst, so much
that she hastened to the edge of death, and life escaped her. And at the
hour of vespers, she entered her cell, and in spirit she said to God:
"Lord, vanquished by your love, you make me endure this fast. Why
do you not remove this pain from me?[6] I am a woman and a sinner.
Why do you forsake me?[7] You were put to the torment of the cross
for the sake of sinners." And suddenly, the servant of God saw a multitude of people, running together with pitchers of water and wine.
And a golden cup, full of water and wine, was put to her mouth. And
that evening, her sisters, visiting her and guarding her in the cell, saw
her body greatly enlarged, as if she were pregnant, and [they saw that]
her face, which first had been blackened and made dark through
refusing to drink, regained its color, shining and serene. And all
that night, she remained in contemplation. And similarly, the following night, her heart was in contemplation. Then a silver tube was
put to her mouth, from which sweetness and wonderful smoothness
issued. And such sweet liqueur was drawn from the tube that the elements of her body could hardly stay together.

62. Three days from then,[8] she was again raised up, and a real mirror was presented to her, which illuminated all [the women] with its
own clarity. Many people gathered to see it, peasant women and
women from far away. They attracted and received rays of clarity from
both the right and the left, and prayers and life issued from this mirror.[9] And when she returned to herself, her eyes, due to the excess of
light and clarity, remained for three days without seeing the sunlight.
Lady Druditia, Agnes, Amata, Nicoluccia, and Catherina testified
about this to the other sisters.

63. And again, when her body grew and became so large, there
could be witnesses of this, because they made themselves known
openly. And from the time of this wonderful drink onward, she did
not drink water or wine for about eleven years, except when she took
communion.[10] And then her heart grew to such a height of charity

[and] entered into such a fervent love that, as for her, she supremely honored, praised, and glorified God. And she was always more ardent and desirous that the happy good things she experienced might be tasted again, and especially by her dear male and female friends, fellow citizens, and familiar acquaintances. And she brought it about so that they would come to know the Lord.

64. Once, while praying to God fervently and with all her heart, with all the highest love she prayed to her sweet Lord for herself and others. She spoke with great affection, saying, "I know that, as humbly as I can, my Lord, I pray to you that you enter into the heart of these creatures and cause them to feel how sweet and worthy of love you are; that, through your love, you may cleanse them of all meanness and dishonesty and free them from all ties to the world." While she prayed like this with insistence and fervor, from the altar, on which there was a little painting where Christ our Lord was depicted, she heard a voice that spoke to her thus: "It is not proper that you call to me with such insistence and so strenuously for what you ask and desire. But believe and trust firmly that we will inscribe these people, whom you love, in the book of life."

65. And our Lord allowed that all her delights refer to the cross, to which her heart was always directed with unbelievable ardor and in which it rested, all inflamed. And the sharp martyrdoms that our Lord suffered were present for her, as though she saw all of them. And for fifteen days, it lasted that the servant of God, with the eyes of her own body, saw Christ crucified in the flesh as a man; how his hands and feet were fixed with piercing nails and his side was pierced with the lance and gravely wounded.

66. While she was still praying in her cell and attending fervently to prayer, our Lord appeared to her with white clothing and with a joyful countenance, with golden hair shining beyond measure,[11] so that the human tongue would not be able to relate it. And when she wanted to seize him, she was struck dumb with fear, and she wondered if she was not deceived by the tricks of the demon. And so she spoke in this way: "I praise that Lord who came down from heaven to earth and was made flesh in the Virgin Mary and remained hidden for nine months in the womb of that Virgin. And I praise and adore that Lord

who, out of his own humility, wanted to be born in the manger, between the donkey and the ox. I praise and adore Jesus Christ crucified, who lived for thirty years in this world and wanted to live among
sinners and who suffered hunger and sweat and endured cold. And I
praise and adore him who was betrayed by Judas Iscariot and sentenced to the cross for the sake of sinners, dragged by a halter and
beaten at the column and crowned with thorns, and who let himself
be led to Mount Calvary, reserved for thieves." After saying these
words, she showed great delight. And Jesus Christ said to her, "And I
am he, and my side was pierced by the lance."[12] And he disappeared.
And the woman remained consoled. And Sister Druditia, who was
outside by the cell door, heard many of Sister Clare's words.

67. A few days later, while she was engaged in some physical tasks,
the most blessed Virgin appeared to her. And the servant of God
wondered whether this was not a deception of the demon, but it was
verified by very definite and very evident signs. And she remained
with her for a long time.

68. She rejoiced greatly in divine offices, and especially in the Gospel, because they were the words of Christ and, above all, in the
Gospel of the *multitude* fed by the *five loaves and two fishes*,[13] which it
gave her great pleasure to hear. And entering the garden with the
sisters, she was raised up in such contemplation that she seemed to
see the Lord really present, multiplying the loaves and the fish and
ordering the apostles to place them before the multitude, and in the
same way [she saw] the other things that are written there in order.
And she saw these things while remaining kneeling the whole time.
And similarly, seven of her sisters remained on bended knee with
her the whole time.

69. Finally, on the feast of St. Lucy,[14] this chosen and cherished servant of God was conjoined with our Lord in such exceedingly great
divine contemplation that she lost all her bodily senses. And speaking with the sisters, she seemed to be a most pure lamb and a girl of
twelve years,[15] as though she had been restored to a state of innocence.
And she remained like this for six months, as though deprived of her
bodily senses. In the end, her other senses returned to her; only the
sense of sight did not return to her so that she could open her eyes.

And indeed, if she opened them, she would immediately close them. She did not interact with people, or speak to them.

70. Among the other things and pains that she endured, she was tormented by thirst an infinite number of times, and it seemed that she would surely be overcome by this thirst and her body would dissolve into its primal elements. This was not a thirst that she could quench or that could be overcome by drinking water or wine. And many times, she tried to drink and taste water, yet the more she drank, the more the thirst tormented her. For this was a thirst for the blood of Christ and the immaculate Lamb. She had a thirst for this blood, and she longingly asked and desired that all the fountains, streams, and waters that she had seen would turn into the blood of the Lord. But when she had taken the flesh and blood of our Lord,[16] suddenly, by this fact, the burning and unbelievable thirst ceased. Because of this, as a wise and discerning person, she wanted to clarify whether this was ever found in sacred scripture. And so she sent to beg Sir Girolamo, bishop of Rimini, from whom she had received many counsels, that he might deign to come to her. And when he had come to her, she begged him and asked if in divine scripture anything appeared in writing about such a thirst. And he said that the prophet Jeremiah said: "There will be again people who will have *not a thirst* of *wine* or *of water*, but this will be a thirst for the immaculate Lamb."[17] And from then on, she remained in a state of clarity.[18]

*   *   *

The *Life of Clare* comprises twelve chapters in all. These chapter divisions were the work of the original hagiographer (several times, he writes, "and to conclude this chapter"), not a later imposition. Nor was twelve a random number. The monastic office of matins, which illustrates the life of the saint whose feast is to be celebrated that day, comprises twelve readings recited from about 3 AM to dawn. Thus to divide a hagiographic text into twelve pieces is to suggest the possibility of liturgical use in case of eventual canonization; our hagiographer was thinking ahead.

But for now, we arrive at his final chapter, and the end of Clare's life seems to draw near. A reference (paragraph 63) to events said to have occurred at least eleven years before Clare's death reminds us that not everything in this chapter should be understood as occurring in her last days. Still, Clare now seems immobilized, stationary in her community, driven only by several remaining elements that reduce her experience to its very essence: demonic temptation, visionary experience of the Passion, and hunger and thirst for the body and blood of Christ. These themes weave in and out of a concluding chapter that alternates between suffering and delight, between tension and release.

We have seen Clare attacked by hostile preachers, skeptical neighbors, and even rebellious sisters. Now only a final enemy remains: demons. Our hagiographer has already shown Clare tempted by demons (Chapter 3) and even accused of being a demon herself (Chapter 6). The decades of Clare's adulthood, from the 1280s through the 1320s, witnessed a growing fascination with the demonic among learned churchmen, as though demons had somehow been set loose to wreak havoc with the European imagination. Would-be holy women were increasingly expected to suffer their attacks; a controversial figure such as Ermine of Reims (c. 1347–c. 1396) would eventually be written about as though her holiness consisted almost entirely of fending off their never-ending offensive. The final chapter of the *Life of Clare* seems to presage this development, as demons thread into and out of the narrative.

Clare's temptation has an explicit sexual element. These evil spirits that promise to "enter on top of" her threaten her as *incubi*; that is, demons in male form that solicit and seduce women, often in their sleep. Thus their temptation challenges Clare's hard-won chastity. These demonic attacks, however, ultimately serve precisely to prove Clare's "worthiness." Demons might be satanic spirits, but the devil could act only with God's permission, as the book of Job (1:12) made clear. If Clare endures this challenge, it is because "God permits it" according to his "will." And if demons single out Clare for vexation, it is because she is imbued with particular holiness and is thus a worthwhile target. The mere fact that Clare understands and declares this reality is enough to drive off the demons, at least momentarily. When their attacks resume, they cause Clare such severe falls that she damages a leg and even apparently loses a finger. But after her sisters rally around her—again, serving to restore cohesion to the recently fractured community—"God himself lifted all the demons' harassments from her."

Clare's visions and vexations increasingly come with precise liturgical dates (though not exact years) and with more extensive lists of witnesses—again, an indication that possible canonization hearings were at least in the back of our hagiographer's mind. On the vigil of the feast of Mary Magdalene (July 21), Clare experiences an episode of ecstatic contemplation, witnessed by Sisters Amata and Viola. Clare is so deep in rapture that "she totally lost the power of speech." Clare has already been deprived of a finger and walks with the aid of a cane, and now she even has trouble speaking. We sense that she is reaching the end of her strength.

The feast of the conversion of St. Paul (January 25) naturally causes Clare to return to another crucial element of her own conversion: the rejection of food and drink. But more than hunger, it is thirst that now tortures her. In her torment and guilt, she seems to doubly blame herself: "I am a woman and a sinner!" Like Christ, she cries out, "Why do you forsake me?" In response, a golden cup full of water and wine miraculously appears. But instead of simply slaking her thirst, the drink makes Clare's body grow, "as if she were pregnant." Indeed, it lends her a healthy radiance, the way pregnant women are often said to glow. The relief continues the next night, when a "silver tube is put to her mouth," filling her body with "sweet liqueur." Clare thus experiences both a purification and something like a "mystical" or "spiritual" pregnancy. This phenomenon in holy women's spirituality was most famously experienced by Birgitta of Sweden (c. 1303–1373), a Scandinavian noblewoman who spent much of her later life in Rome. Birgitta, unlike Clare, was a mother, and so knew exactly how an actual pregnancy felt.

For Clare, the experience is related to her earlier sensation (reported by our hagiographer in Chapters 5 and 11) of having a small child "tied to her heart." These experiences represent an identification with Mary and the virgin birth. Clare's vision—or, at least, our hagiographer's description—is also eroticized, with the "silver tube" and its "sweet liqueur" not only leaving her as though pregnant but producing in her body such "sweetness and wonderful smoothness . . . that the elements of her body could hardly stay together." Medieval authors, churchmen like Bernard of Clairvaux as well as beguines like Hadewijch of Brabant, frequently used the language of sexual satisfaction to describe the intense pleasure of the divine presence and the language of frustrated longing to describe its absence. Modern readers sometimes try to convince themselves that such a spiritual discourse hides a subconscious sexual reality. The temptation is to think that our modern perspective has uncovered the "real" meaning behind the eroticized imagery. In fact, there is nothing hidden or subconscious about it; in medieval texts such as this, an explicit sexual discourse expresses a powerful spiritual experience.

Three days later, Clare sees the miraculous apparition of a radiant mirror, witnessed by "Lady Druditia," along with Agnes, Amata, Nicoluccia, and Catherina. This mirror—representing God, the source of all light—shines so brightly that Clare is blinded for three days. As a result of these episodes, for eleven years Clare would not drink wine, except when she took communion. The Eucharist remained, to the end, at the center of her devotions. We recall in Chapter 4 how Clare collapsed in the Dominican church of Rimini, only to be revived when Brother Girolamo, future bishop of Rimini, gave her the Host. From that point on, Clare's confessions and communions only became more frequent and intense. For medieval Christians, the Eucharist was, in the most literal and physical sense, the body of Christ, as the Fourth Lateran Council of 1215 had affirmed. To attend Mass was to "see the Savior," as he became present in the Host. To take communion was to ingest the body of Christ. If Clare, at moments of intense visionary contemplation, could feel herself to have the Christ child within her, she could also feel Christ enter her body every time she took communion. As Caroline Bynum has demonstrated, tasting, chewing, and swallowing the Eucharist was a kind of holy feast that balanced, for many holy women, the holy fast of denying the body more ordinary kinds of food.

After the Fourth Lateran Council had declared that all the faithful were required to confess and take communion once a year, holy women quickly began to clamor for more frequent access to the body of Christ. Margherita of Cortona, for instance, wanted to take communion every day, but her confessor would allow it only once a month. In a vision, Christ intervened to grant her what she sought (though she later renounced the privilege out of humility). Indeed, it was a holy woman, Juliana of Cornillon, who inspired and promoted the annual feast of Corpus Christi, approved by Pope Urban IV in 1264.

Yet the church also began to reserve the sacrament "in both kinds" for priests alone; that is, the laity would be offered the wafer, but only the officiating priest sipped the wine. This restriction helped foster a fascination with—indeed, a longing for—the blood of Christ among devout laypeople. Christ's wounds become ever more visible in late medieval art, where painters seem to compete to see which Crucifixion scene can most vividly depict the fountain of blood pouring from the hands, feet, and side of the Savior. Sometimes, such scenes even include angels holding chalices to catch the precious blood, as in Giotto's painting for the north transept of the lower church of San Francesco in Assisi.

Stories of miracles (often with hideously anti-Jewish morals) likewise describe consecrated wafers as bleeding if stabbed, thereby demonstrating the invisible fact of their transformation into the body of the Christ. Clare's thirst for the blood of Christ is part and parcel of these trends. Remarkably, however, she has a remedy at hand. The text is perfectly clear: she did not drink wine for eleven years, "except when she took communion." Clare, then, took communion in both kinds. This new transgression is among the most surprising in a text full of such indiscretions. How did she persuade a priest— perhaps her confessor—to give her access to the forbidden chalice? Our author is silent.

To the end, Clare continues her practice of meditating on images (her loss of sight being, for now, only temporary). Praying before an altar on behalf of "others" too prone to "meanness and dishonesty," a voice from "a little painting where Christ our Lord was depicted" gently chastises her for making such insistent demands. Eventually, Christ relents and promises to inscribe Clare's friends "in the book of life." If that voice is uncharacteristically disembodied, Clare's visions soon return to "the sharp martyrdoms that our Lord suffered," which seem to float before her eyes. For fifteen days, she sees "with the eyes of her own body" Christ crucified on the cross, wounded in the hands, feet, and side. His blood, we can assume, flowed freely.

While Clare is "still" praying in her cell, the Lord appears to her, clothed in white and with a joyful countenance, his "golden hair shining beyond measure." The "still" (or "again," *anchora*) suggests that this new episode is part of the same sequence of events, which now veers into apocalyptic imagery. The golden hair and white clothing may be an inverted echo of a passage in St. John's Apocalypse (1:13–14) where Christ ("the Son of Man") appears with a golden belt and white hair. Fearful, Clare again suspects that this apparition could be the trick of "the demon," which is only to be expected as the End and the Second Coming approach. In the face of this doubt, Clare is forced to "prove" the vision by reciting her own elaborate statement of faith, centered on the birth and death of Christ; for Clare, as for many contemporary holy women, resurrection and ascension seem less important than incarnation and the Passion. Like a kind of exorcism, her passionate creed dispels demonic doubt—but not for long: only a few days later, "the most blessed Virgin appeared to her. And the servant of God wondered whether this was not a deception of the demon." This time, the vision is "verified by very definite and very evident signs," though we are not told what they are.

No such doubt about possible demonic deception has been ascribed to Clare's visions in earlier chapters. Suddenly, Clare seems on guard; or, at least, her hagiographer is wary on her behalf. As is so often the case, our text seems prescient. In an increasingly demon-filled spiritual landscape, it would become essential for holy women to be able to "discern" whether a vision or voice came from God or from Satan. By the end of the fourteenth century, dubious churchmen tended more and more to suspect that unsettling visions reported by disorderly women were likely to be demonic deceptions rather than divine gifts. By around 1400, a whole genre of "discernment of spirits" treatises began to appear, written by learned men who portrayed malleable women as particularly susceptible to demonic tricks. Consequently, confessors and other churchmen writing about holy women began to try to head off challenges in advance. For example, when Raymond of Sabanac recorded the controversial visions of Constance of Rabastens around 1386, he made sure to begin with a mini-treatise on discerning demonic from divine visions, preemptively reassuring readers that Constance's revelations fit his criteria for the latter. More subtly, a decade later, when Jean le Graveur wrote about Ermine of Reims, he portrayed her as questioning and testing nearly every vision that she experienced, out of a constant suspicion that what seemed to be the apparition of a saint might really be a demonic delusion. The saintly woman herself should show humble doubt about her worthiness to receive divine inspiration. Clare and her hagiographer, as early as the 1320s, seem to point toward this heightened fear of demonic delusion.

"Finally," on the Feast of St. Lucy (December 13), Clare is so fully joined to the Lord that "she lost all her bodily senses." In this condition, she can be neither tempted nor deceived, thus resolving the tensions threaded throughout the chapter. Clare remains in a state of total innocence, deprived of her senses, for six months. Eventually, her other senses return, but not her sight; indeed, she can hardly open her eyes. There is an inverse relationship to the usual role of the ancient martyr Lucy. Her name derives from the Latin *lux*, or light; during her own martyrdom, she was said to have had her eyes plucked out. Thus St. Lucy's intervention was often sought by those who suffered from eye problems. In Clare's case, however, under Lucy's patronage her sight slips away, turning inward. Clare now sees the world only as "through a glass darkly" (1 Cor. 13:12) like St. Paul, or like Dante, through "a kind of white haze" (*Convivio* III, ix, 15).

As sight and sound fade, only thirst remains. Clare's earlier vision of water and wine miraculously flowing from a golden cup had temporarily lessened this sensation. But now, no amount of water or wine can quench her thirst "for the blood of Christ and the immaculate Lamb," which burns so insistently that she longs for Rimini's fountains to run with the "blood of the Lord." Communion in both kinds—the wafer and the wine, the body and the blood— is the only remedy that can cool her thirst, just as the Host had restored her to health in the Dominican church of Rimini many years ago. Clare, always imbued with a scholar's impulse to find justification in the word of God and assurance that her life conforms to God's will, wonders whether such a thirst has ever been attested in scripture. And so she sends word to Bishop Girolamo of Rimini that she wishes him to come to her.

The Dominican Girolamo had good reason to understand her longing; he was the very same man who had cured her earlier collapse by giving her the Host (in Chapter 4). But that interaction had occurred when he was merely prior of the Dominican convent, long before his investment as bishop in March 1323. He was then merely "a certain Brother Girolamo"; he is now "Sir (*messere*) Girolamo." Apparently, he had kept up his relationship with Clare over the years, even as his career took off. In Chapter 4, we saw reference to him hearing Clare's confession; now he is said to offer her "many counsels." The strength of these ties is demonstrated by the fact that he comes when Clare calls. Her question is simple enough: Does anything like such a thirst appear in scripture?

Our hagiographer's report of the bishop's answer is rather perplexing. Bishop Girolamo replies that the prophet Jeremiah predicted that there would be people who would thirst not for wine or water but "for the immaculate Lamb." The book of Jeremiah, however, contains no such prophecy. Instead, the phrase seems to be based on a passage from the book of Amos (8:11): "Behold the days come, says the Lord, and I will send forth a famine into the land: not a famine of bread, nor a thirst of water, but of hearing the word of the Lord." The passage is mingled with one from St. John's Apocalypse (7:14–17): "These are they who are come out of great tribulation . . . and have made them white in the blood of the Lamb. . . . They shall no more hunger nor thirst. . . . For the Lamb, which is in the midst of the throne, shall rule them, and shall lead them to the fountains of the waters of life."

In one sense, the bishop's response teaches Clare nothing. She already knows full well that her thirst is for the blood of Christ, "the immaculate Lamb." But she is reassured; such thirst is part of God's plan, prophesied in the Old Testament. Despite the apparent confusion in Girolamo's reference, Clare can find certainty in this textual verification. "The word of the Lord," as much as the "blood of the Lamb," has been Clare's obsession, to preach and teach in the streets of Rimini, to dispute with learned masters, to interpret for her sisters. In her climactic vison of St. John in Chapter 11, he held out to her a book, the gift from Christ himself of a kind of literacy at one remove. Clare never wrote anything herself, as far as we know. But her hagiographer, here at the very end of his work, assures us that just as her thirst for the blood of Christ is finally sated through the Eucharist, so her thirst for the word of God is confirmed in her final conference with her old friend the bishop Girolamo.

* * *

Here the original text of *The Life of the Blessed Clare* leaves off, with a kind of "happily ever after": "And from then on, she remained in a state of clarity" (*Et da quel poi dichiarata remase*). Clare's journey has led from luxurious marriage to harsh penitence, from a rain-soaked cell to a thriving community. It has included exile and travel, veneration and excoriation, humility and rebellion, visions and miracles, preaching and performing—most importantly, in the streets of Rimini but also on the road to Assisi. Yet, as our hagiographer's last little pun insists, through it all she remained *dichiarata*; "clarified" or "in a state of clarity," but also "Clare-ified," made and declared to be clearly and completely Clare.

Clare's story, in its totality, underlines the impossibility of resolving long-running historical debates as to whether the Christian religion advanced or limited women's roles in medieval society. Women in Italian city-states and elsewhere in medieval Europe faced challenges, but their weakness could be their force, and their simplicity could be their sophistication. They commanded the attention of their companions, stirred up crowds, challenged the politically powerful, intrigued priests, engaged the learned, and conversed with bishops and cardinals. At heart, the source of Clare's certainty was simple. Clare understood better than others the power of redemption, because she felt more fully its necessity.

Death, *Life*, Afterlife

[Addition at the end of the manuscript]: And supported in this manner,[1] she finally arrived at her death, the end that awaits all the living. As it approached, she preached the word of God to her dear little sisters, exhorting them to peace, charity, fervor of spirit, and to the contemplation of death, and all this with clarity of voice and serenity of countenance. And as she relinquished her spirit, to unite it to the choir of angels and to enjoy celestial goods, she spoke these words to her Lord: "To you, O Lord, *into your hands I commend my spirit.*"[2] Thus she expired from this miserable world and began to live in heaven in that life that will have no end. And as a true indication of her blessedness and true repose, this dead body did not look like a cadaver, as all the dead usually do, full of stench and stink. Instead, with sweet smell and radiant color, it seemed like an ornate garden, full of white lilies and bright red roses.[3] When it was known that Sister Clare was dead, all the people of Rimini came running, weeping so intensely that it cannot be described. It appeared to everyone that this dead woman had sped her steps to raise to the eyes of the living this bright clarity, from which the city received such benefits and bounty through her saintly words of exhortation, infinite charity, and effective examples of goodness and full of all virtue.[4]

71. The above-mentioned saintly lady Sister Clare died in the year of the Lord 1346, on the tenth day of February.[5]

[Addition at the beginning of the manuscript]. Because of her abstinence, she seemed like a shadow; she was destroyed, pale, and indeed so weakened, so worn out and deprived of human strength, that she could hardly draw her own breath. Nevertheless, not for herself but for the other poor, knocking door-to-door, she sought alms for charity, preaching to the rich and greedy that "alms-giving is the treasure with which the debt of sins is paid[6] and the key to opening paradise,[7] the *precious pearl*,[8] the oil of the Shunammite,[9] the wheat of the widow of Sareptha,[10] the ointment of the Magdalen,[11] the ladder of Jacob,[12] and the tunic of Jesus Christ.[13] That is why you should cheerfully give alms, because it is as useful to you as oil is to the lamp, sun to the day, a flake to ice, and air to the body. Do not regret to give alms! Open your granaries and help the poor, O my people of Rimini!"[14]

*   *   *

Clare "at last arrived at her death." But when, and how? One of the most remarkable facts about the *Life of Clare* is that, in its original form, it ends without describing its subject's death or burial. The story that begins this Epilogue was clearly not the work of our hagiographer. It was added to our unique manuscript in the second half of the sixteenth century, perhaps a hundred years after the manuscript was first copied. It evidently attempts to supply several expected items that are conspicuously missing from the end of the narrative. Thus we find a few lines about Clare's good death, which represent her as reciting Christ's own dying words and offering a pious example for her sisters. There is an obligatory statement about the saintly body smelling of roses, and two concluding sentences about Rimini's collective sense of loss. None of this is very precise. Likewise, the single sentence that forms paragraph 71 must have been composed long after Clare's lifetime, perhaps when our manuscript was copied in the second half of the fifteenth century. The date it gives for Clare's death, February 10, 1346, cannot be correct. Clare's community did later celebrate her memory on February 10, so the day itself may be accurate. But the year must be about two decades too late.

Why does our hagiographer, in his original text, not provide the expected description of Clare's deathbed, the scene of her burial, and a list of accompanying miracles, as one usually finds at the end of a saint's life? The most likely answer is quite simple, though highly unusual in the hagiographic tradition: Clare's *Life* was written while she was still alive. Such a scenario is very rare in medieval hagiography, but there are other examples. The most famous is Sulpicious Severus's life of Martin of Tours (d. 397); centuries later, the life of Christina of Markyate (d. c. 1155) seems to have been begun before her death; and Goswin of Bossut's life of the monk Abundus was written before his death, around 1239. Certainly, it was not unheard of for those around a would-be saint to begin taking notes for a potential life during the subject's lifetime. Bernard of Clairvaux's secretaries undoubtedly copied down his sayings, and there are indications that Margherita Colonna's brothers were gathering material for a life as she suffered through her last illness in 1280.

If our interpretation is correct, we can offer a plausible reconstruction of how *The Life of the Blessed Clare of Rimini* came into existence. The final scene in the original text (the end of Chapter 12) can be fixed fairly precisely, since Girolamo Fisici was bishop of Rimini only from March 1323 to September 1328. In Chapter 3, we have seen some indication that Clare lived until at least 1324, when she would have been about sixty-four years old. She was clearly in decline by this point; some of the last scenes recorded in the *Life* show her bedridden and without the use of her senses for a full six months. Clare cannot have lived long beyond her reassuring conference with Bishop Girolamo. We can assume that she died on February 10, in a year between 1324 and 1329.

So we can picture the scene. Sometime in these years, Bishop Girolamo is summoned to Clare's bedside. She asks her fervent but unexpected question about biblical precedents for her burning thirst. Girolamo, searching his memory, gives a soothing, if not textually precise, answer. The exchange moves him. He has known Clare for years and watched her career through all its triumphs and tribulations. Now he sees that she cannot have long to live. He confers with her confessor about her exceptional life. The Dominican and the Franciscan find that they are in agreement: it would be worthwhile to gather the memories of the sisters and others who knew Clare. Formal canonization might be an unlikely prospect, but in the heightened emotional context of Clare's last months on earth, it must have seemed like a pious duty to begin to construct a "life" that would serve as an example to others, especially "vain ladies."

Although the foregoing reconstruction is speculative, there is every reason to think that the bishop and the confessor would have agreed on the utility of recording Clare's *Life*. Girolamo Fisici's period as bishop did not leave a strong mark in the records of Rimini, beyond five surviving papal letters directed to him. But he does appear in an intriguing second hagiographic dossier, this one of a local Dominican named Simon (1271–c. 1329), a nearly exact contemporary of Clare. After joining the Dominicans around 1298, Simon devoted himself to penitential fasts and self-flagellation. He suffered demonic attacks, was reassured by visions and celestial voices, and even venerated an image of John the Evangelist. Simon seems in obvious ways to be a male, Dominican analogue to Clare's female, Franciscan-leaning career. Bishop Girolamo shows up in this second work of hagiography as he prepares to inaugurate a new monastery for the Dominican sisters of Rimini in 1326, just about the time of Clare's death. St. Catherine miraculously appears to Simon and demands that the new community be dedicated to her, and thus Girolamo Fisici duly consecrates the Dominican nunnery as Santa Caterina. Girolamo's support for both the Dominican sisters and the visionary, ascetic Simon, thus suggests a man who would indeed have wished to promote the possibility of Clare's sanctity.

As for Clare's anonymous confessor, he would have spent years close to Clare and her sisters, administering the sacraments to them, promoting their interests, and protecting their well-being. It was he who would probably have taken charge of the actual writing. Thus while Clare lay on what seemed to be her deathbed, our Franciscan would have set to work, asking the sisters for their memories. He must have turned especially to Clare's biological sister Druditia for information on her early years, but he also gathered statements from the other spiritual sisters about more recent events—just as the sisters of San Damiano had been the main witnesses interviewed for Clare of Assisi's canonization inquiry in 1255. While her confessor took notes and began to put them in order, Clare of Rimini lingered on, not quite ready to give up the ghost. Our hagiographer organized his narrative and put it down on paper or parchment. Perhaps he revised and rewrote. He had heard Clare's confessions, admired her, and learned from her. He must have feared for her safety at times. Now he could craft Clare's experiences into a narrative, explaining her spiritual trajectory to the world.

Many such confessor/holy woman pairs took shape during the High Middle Ages and later, from Jacques of Vitry and Marie of Oignies (d. 1213) to Raymond of Capua and Catherine of Siena (d. 1380) and beyond. As scholars such as John Coakley have demonstrated, the more learned confessor often begins by thinking that he has something to teach the holy woman, but ends up as her spiritual disciple, transfixed by her direct access to God and the revelations that she reports. He lends his Latin literacy and formal learning to their common endeavors, while she supplies the ecstatic experience and charismatic ability to channel the word of God. He interprets and shields her with his written version of her experiences; she provides him with a compelling subject for promotion and commentary. The result is a mutually beneficial collaboration. In this case, however, the confessor chooses to hide his name from history, to disappear into his story and his heroine. Occasionally, he allows himself a general comment on the fickle nature of women or the lures of the world. But his modest humility may be the key to his own daring. From his anonymous perch, he can detail Clare's transgressions, even those that might have reflected poorly on a confessor. In his role as hagiographer, he can have the last word by subtly softening the blow, as we have seen him do so many times.

If the scenario that we have proposed is correct, the *Life of Clare* was never quite finished. Perhaps Clare rallied and lived on for months, or even years, and the momentum was lost. Bishop Girolamo suffered excommunication in the last year of his episcopacy (for a mundane affair of his predecessor's unpaid tithes). Perhaps it was this setback in 1327, or Girolamo's death in 1328, that caused the project to be left incomplete. Beyond pure speculation, all we can say is that the original version of the *Life* never arrived at a report of Clare's death.

The idea that the unfinished *Life* would have been written before Clare died is remarkable. No less noteworthy is the fact that the *Life* seems to have been composed directly in Italian. Saints' lives were traditionally written in Latin, the language of the church. By the early fourteenth century in some parts of Europe, it was not unusual for an older Latin life to be translated into a vernacular language for wider reading; across the Alps, the first saint's life written directly in French—Agnes of Harcourt's *Life of Isabelle of France*—appeared about 1283. In Italy, however, to set down a saint's life directly in the language of everyday speech, the maternal tongue spoken by the common people, remained unheard of in the 1320s.

In Clare's case, we cannot be absolutely certain that there was not also an early attempt to create a Latin life. But no trace of such an effort has ever been found, despite exhaustive searches in the mid-eighteenth century (by Giuseppe Garampi) and the late twentieth (by Jacques Dalarun). As we shall see, the only Latin version that we have is actually an eighteenth-century translation of our very same Italian text. In sum, we know that the *Life* was written in Rimini in the 1320s by an anonymous Franciscan. We know that the earliest surviving version is in Italian, preserved in a unique manuscript of the later fifteenth century. There is no clear evidence to suggest a process of translation from Latin to Italian. The most likely conclusion is that Clare's *Life* was originally written in the vernacular, perhaps because our hagiographer was writing for a community of laywomen unversed in Latin.

In our surviving manuscript, the north Italian language of the *Life* shows few strong regional characteristics, though there are occasional indications of Venetian and Romagnolo (the dialect of the Romagna). It may be that the fifteenth-century copyist was Venetian, or that he or she received his or her training in a school in the larger region around Padua and Venice. Venetian dialect was, in any case, a familiar presence in the port of Rimini, as it was in other ports on the Adriatic coast. The grammar of the text is fluent, lexical repetitions are rare, and the archaic elements are few. The *Life* has an elegant literary character that shows a certain level of refinement. If he really wrote directly in Italian, our original author was an unheralded literary pioneer. Dante Alighieri was his contemporary, having only recently died in 1321, in nearby Ravenna. Dante's *On Vernacular Eloquence* (*De Vulgari Eloquentia*, 1303–1305) broke new ground in theorizing the use of the common tongue on the Italian peninsula, a promise fulfilled in Dante's own masterwork, *The Divine Comedy* (completed 1320–1321). Following in this illustrious wake, our anonymous Franciscan seems to have dared to use Italian to capture the immediacy of Clare's words and experiences. Clare's *Life* is a valuable witness not only to her religious, political, and social world but to the development of the vernacular language that (along with Dante's Tuscan) would become the Italian still in use today.

It is important to note that the Italian language flourished in poetry before it did in prose. Indeed, Italian poetry was born around 1224 with Francis of Assisi, the founder of the Franciscan order, and his *Canticle of Brother Sun*. In the following years, the vernacular developed at the Sicilian school of Frederick II's court in Palermo and reached its apex at the end of the thirteenth century, in Florence, with Dante and the Stilnovisti, a group of poets whose "sweet new style" eventually came to embody the innovative Italian sound. The new vernacular refined itself through poetry first, where it found its harmony before it was used in prose. In his masterpiece, *The Decameron* (1349–1353), Giovanni Boccaccio finally formulated the new Italian vernacular into a narrative language, in what can be considered the first modern novel. If we look closely at our hagiographer's use of language and consider the period in which he wrote, we may fully appreciate his innovations in moving away from the literal style of treatises, and from biblical mannerism, toward the refined grace found in humanistic narratives of the Italian Renaissance.

The elegant linguistic quality of this hagiography is extremely fine and seems ahead of contemporary Tuscan chronicles. It can be considered a unique example in its own time. The prose presents a mix of modern narrative and poetic language, which offers a new and unexpected example of Italian vernacular refinement. In the same way as poetry in the new Italian vernacular was born with Francis, using the Umbrian vernacular in a sophisticated way, we can argue that vernacular prose also developed thanks to this *Life* written by a Franciscan (for and with a female community), which anticipates many literary developments to come.

* * *

If Clare's confessor, her community, or her bishop thought of pursing her canonization, any such idea must have been short-lived. Not only was her *Life* left unfinished; in the 1320s, a controversial holy woman tinged with Spiritual Franciscan sympathies could hardly have expected an enthusiastic hearing at John XXII's increasingly repressive curia. Clare of Montefalco, promoted by Cardinal Napoleone Orsini, had received a formal inquiry into her case for sanctity beginning in 1317, but even after a favorable opinion was given by three cardinals in 1331, John declined to canonize her. This was the period in which Peter of John Olivi's works were formally condemned (1326), and his most radical followers, such as Na Prous Boneta, were arrested (1325) and burned at the stake (1328). A quick canonization was never in the cards for Clare of Rimini.

But if Clare never achieved the wider fame of a canonized saint, she was not soon forgotten in Rimini. We have seen (in Chapter 11) that two stunning triptychs were created between about 1330 and 1350, drawing on our hagiographic legend as their inspiration. These paintings were made for and displayed in Clare's community, which, at least by 1457, had come to be known as Santa Maria degli Angeli (like the Portiuncula, which Clare had visited outside Assisi). Twenty-four surviving documents mention the community between 1329 and 1481, and, at least up until 1377, they always refer to it as founded by "Sister Clare." This community must also have preserved Clare's unfinished *Life*, in whatever state the hagiographer left it. His original manuscript no longer survives, but a new copy—the one that remains today—was made at Santa Maria degli Angeli in the second half of the fifteenth century (see Figure 8).

Even this copy of the *Life* long remained slightly unfinished, with the initial letters of each chapter left to be filled in. It was only decades later, about the time that the community became a more formal house of Franciscan nuns in 1522, that modestly ornamented capitals were added to the manuscript. Later in the sixteenth century, the short addition supplying expected details on Clare's death (the beginning of our Epilogue) was added.

At about the same time, someone at Santa Maria degli Angeli used the inside of the opening flyleaf to copy (also in Italian) an intriguing story about Clare's preaching. We might hesitate before accepting this late addition as direct evidence of Clare's real actions. Yet it rings true to what we know of Clare's career. Pale, weak, and worn out, Clare goes door-to-door to beg alms for others. Remarkably, both sixteenth-century additions to the manuscript refer specifically to Clare "preaching"—in this instance, using a pastiche of biblical phrases to shame the "rich and greedy" into giving generously, if only to assure their own salvation. If it can be trusted, it is one last example of Clare's fearless forays into the streets, proclaiming the word of God to "my people of Rimini."

*   *   *

In the years after 1522, a certain amount of historical confusion crept into memories of Clare's career. For one thing, there was a natural tendency to assert, in retrospect, that she had been a Franciscan nun or tertiary. For another, there was an attempt to add to her luster by making her a member of the powerful Agolanti family (twenty-first-century websites still perpetuate these errors). But confusion or no, several abortive efforts proposed her as a candidate for beatification in the seventeenth century, in the era when beatification emerged as a way to recognize locally venerated figures who did

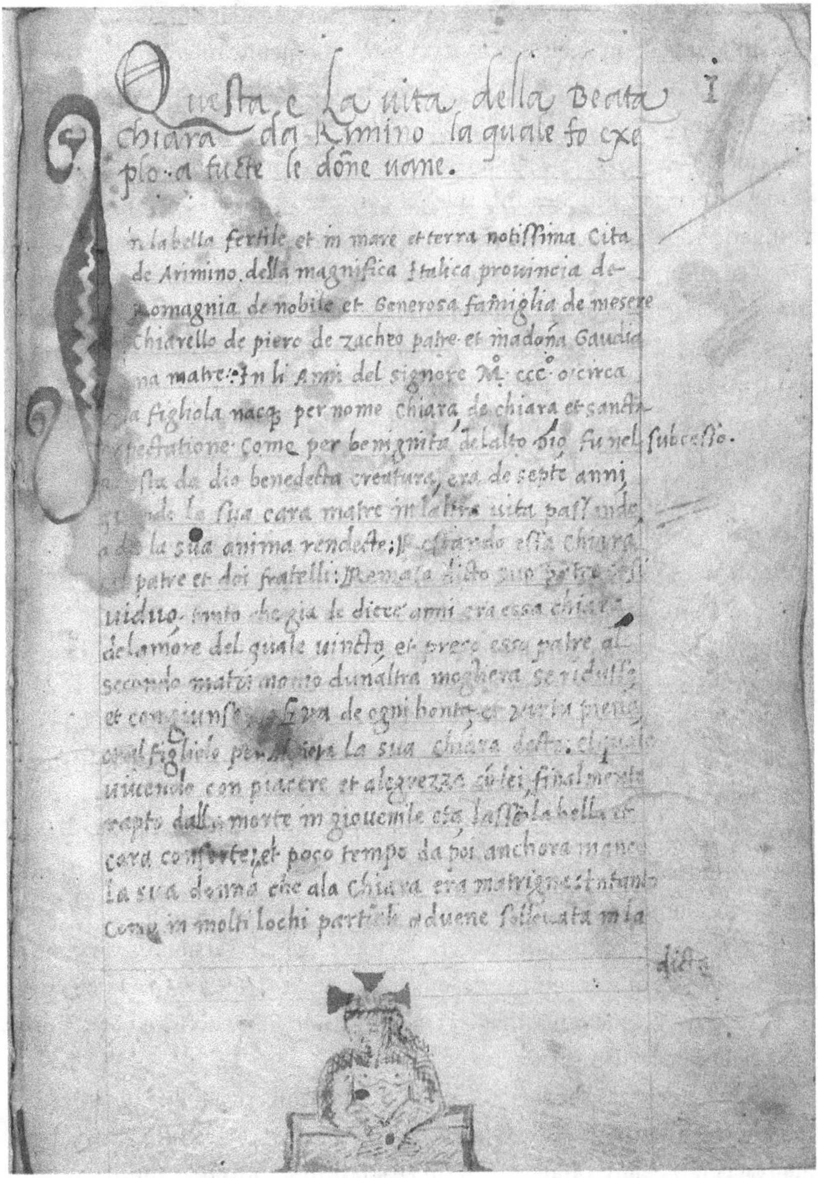
Questa e La uita della Beata chiara da Rimino la quale fo exeplo a tutte le done nome. I

In la bella fertile et in mare et terra notissima Cita de Arimino della magnifica Italica provincia de Romagnia de nobile et Generosa famiglia de mesere Chiarello de piero de zacheo patre et madona Gaudia sua matre: In li Anni del signore M ccc o circa una fighiola nacq per nome chiara de chiara et sancta expectatione

Figure 8. First page of the unique manuscript of *The Life of the Blessed Clare of Rimini*. Rimini, Biblioteca del Seminario Vescovile, MS 144, fol. 1r. Used by permission of the Archivio Storico Diocesano di Rimini.

not rise to the level of inclusion in the universal calendar of saints. At last, in the enlightened eighteenth century, Clare's moment came. In 1751, the miraculous cure of a sister of Santa Maria degli Angeli named Maria Vittoria drew the attention of church officials. Clare's cause was taken up by Giuseppe Garampi (1725–1792), a brilliant scholar (and future cardinal) from Rimini who was charged with heading the Vatican archives. He based his initial investigations on our manuscript, the unique surviving copy of Clare's Italian *Life*. Garampi was the first to edit and publish the text, in his monumental *Memorie ecclesiastiche appartenenti all'istoria e al culto della B. Chiara di Rimini* (Rome, 1755; see Figure 9). He showed that the supposed link to the Agolanti family was a mistake, proved that Clare had never been a Franciscan nun or tertiary, and argued that indeed the *Life* had first been written in Italian. If Garampi's impressive scholarship had been allowed to stand unchallenged, a great deal of later confusion could have been avoided. Alas, a long and complicated debate with several intellectual adversaries ensued, with disputes over the authenticity and importance of various accounts of Clare's life. At one point, this virulent counterattack even included Garampi's opponents producing a forged life, supposedly written in secret characters said to resemble Hebrew.

Finally, in 1781, a beatification process was opened. The *Life of Clare* was included in the dossier compiling evidence for her cause, but silently translated into Latin, as though seeking to hide the fact that the original hagiographer had used the less prestigious vernacular. Moreover, this Latin version quietly omitted certain parts of the *Life*, which happened to be the most controversial moments in Clare's career, such as the accusation of heresy. Nevertheless, despite continuing uncertainty as to which version or versions of Clare's *Life* was or were authentic, on November 16, 1785, Clare was beatified by Pope Pius VI, meaning that a local cult could be established and a feast day celebrated in Rimini.

Clare's glory was short-lived. Santa Maria degli Angeli was destroyed in 1810, in the aftermath of the Napoleonic invasions. Thankfully, the unique manuscript of Clare's Italian *Life* survived. It first moved to the archives of the cathedral chapter of Rimini and then joined the collection of the episcopal seminary in the same city, where it remains today. Clare's relics underwent a similar journey. In 1810, her body was moved to the church of the former Franciscan convent of the city, the famous Tempio Malatestiano con-

QUESTA È LA VITA·
DELLA
BEATA ᵇ CHIARA
DA RIMINO,
LA QUALE FO ᵈ EXEMPLO A TUTTE
LE DONNE VANE.
CAPO PRIMO.

*Nafcita, educazione, matrimonj, e vita della Beata
fino agli anni 34.*

N la bella, fertile, & in mare ᵉ &
terra notiffima città de Arimino ᶠ,
de la magnifica Italica provincia
de Romagnia ᵍ, de nobile & ge-
nerofa famiglia ʰ de Meffere Chiarello de Piero de Zacheo ⁱ patre,
& Madonna Gaudiana matre, in
li anni del Signore M.° ccc.° o cir-
ca ᴷ, una figliola nacque per nome Chiara, de chiara
& fanᶜta expectatione, como per benignità de l'alto
A   Dio

Figure 9. Opening of the first printed edition of *The Life of the Blessed Clare of Rimini*. Giuseppe Garampi, *Memorie ecclesiastiche appartenenti all'istoria e al culto della B. Chiara di Rimini* (Rome: Pagliarini, 1755). Used by permission of the Silver Special Collections Library, University of Vermont.

ceived by Leon Battista Alberti, which had been designated the cathedral church of Rimini a year earlier, in 1809. There it stayed until World War II. For years, it was thought that her bones must have been incinerated in the bombings of 1944, when the Tempio Malatestiano was partially destroyed. Recently, however, it has come to light that during the war, her relics had been moved for safekeeping to the church of Santa Maria in Corpolò, a small village about twelve kilometers (seven miles) southwest of Rimini. In 2011, these relics were even briefly brought home to Rimini and displayed for a few days at the church of Cristo Re (Christ the King). A scientific examination of the bones at that time confirmed that Clare had lived past the age of fifty. The relics were then returned to Corpolò, where they can be viewed today (see Figure 10).

With her community destroyed, the only manuscript of her Italian *Life* languishing in obscurity, and even her body misplaced, perhaps it is not surprising that modern scholars for a long time showed little interest in

Figure 10. Relics of Clare of Rimini in 2011. Photograph by Stefano De Carolis. Used by permission.

Clare. Pioneering historians of medieval women barely mentioned her in the groundbreaking works of the 1970s and 1980s that established a kind of scholarly canon of medieval female figures. Scholarly interest was further stymied by confusion left over from the muddled battles of the eighteenth century—which text could be trusted to give historians authentic access to Clare's life? In the 1990s, Jacques Dalarun at last took up this challenge and showed beyond doubt that Garampi had been quite right in 1755. The Italian *Life*, likely written while Clare was still alive but preserved only in our late fifteenth-century manuscript, is the first and only medieval life of Clare. After tracking down the modern whereabouts of this manuscript, Dalarun published a critical edition and detailed study in 1994. The translation we have presented here is the first full translation of the *Life of Clare* into any modern language.

*   *   *

For most people today, the Middle Ages evoke images of ignorance, superstition, and brutality. Journalists use "medieval" as convenient shorthand for anything backward, barbaric, or cruel. We seem to need the centuries between antiquity and the Renaissance to be a "Dark Age," so that we can bask in the self-satisfied glow of enlightened modernity.

But in every historical era, daring individuals challenge the established order of things and move history forward. It is not a question of "progress," if that word is meant to imply that human existence inevitably gets better and better over time; rather, it is a question of how change happens and why today is not just a repetition of yesterday. Human history is not cyclical. No human society ever comes back to its starting point. In that sense, history has a forward motion.

The Italian cities of the thirteenth and fourteenth centuries were surely some of the all-time most fertile sites for launching all kinds of historical changes: economic changes based on growing trade and expanding markets, social and political changes with the emergence of communal government, and literary and artistic changes that led to the flourishing culture of the Italian Renaissance. *The Life of the Blessed Clare of Rimini* reflects all this change and packs an extraordinary range of transgressions into a compact text. As a young woman, Clare refused to submit a second time to patriarchal power, and instead chose a husband out of love and desire. Later, from a life of riches and power, she suddenly found herself impoverished and marginalized. But instead of giving up, she drew new energy from this setback and radically reoriented her life, transforming all her earlier tastes for luxury into dramatic acts of penitence. As a widow and an orphan, she declined the protection of her surviving brother. She could have sought security in an established monastic community but chose a solitary life as a recluse in a roofless cell. Having taken this step, she could have been submissive to local churchmen. To the contrary, she often defied their authority and saw herself as the true teacher. She could have remained solitary, but she became the leader of a wider community. She could have meditated quietly in private, but she made herself a riveting public spectacle. Clare adopted the role of a female apostle in the streets of her city. In the end, even that was not enough. Just as Christ became man, in Rimini a woman became a self-proclaimed incarnation of the stigmatized and crucified Christ.

Clare of Rimini pushed the limits of what her society would stand. The whiff of scandal that clung to her life never quite dissipated from her memory, following her into the modern era and relegating her to a modest local cult rather than a glorious canonization. Change does come at a cost. But Clare was always willing to pay.

The Manuscript of *The Life of the Blessed Clare of Rimini*

Description

Rimini, Biblioteca del Seminario Vescovile, MS 144 is a parchment manuscript copied in the second half of the fifteenth century, made up of ii + 28 + ii folios (the bottom portion of fol. 28 is damaged), measuring 206 × 147 mm (approximately 8 by 6 inches). The eighteenth-century binding is wooden boards covered in red morocco leather, with two brass clasps and gilded with iron studs. The twenty-eight central folios comprise two ten-folio quires and one eight-folio quire. Pages are ruled in lead for twenty-seven long lines, and the text is written in a regular humanist hand (the last two lines of each page are always left blank). Three blank lines are left before each new chapter, with the twelve chapters numbered in the margins. Decoration in black ink is limited to initial letters of chapters, added perhaps a half-century after the main text was written.

Fol. ii^r: Episode in the life of Clare of Rimini, in Italian, containing a sermon. Added in the second half of the sixteenth century (translated above, following par. 71).

Fols. 1^r–28^r: Anonymous Italian *Life of the Blessed Clare of Rimini*. Occasional marginal comments by seventeenth- and eighteenth-century hands. Title: *Questa è la vita della beata Chiara da Rimino la quale fo exemplo a tucte le donne vane.*

Fol. 28^{r-v}: Account, in Italian, of the death and burial of Clare of Rimini. Added in the second half of the sixteenth century, with indication that it was to be inserted after par. 70 (where it is translated above).

Fol. iii^{r–v}: Latin hymn of twenty-four verses in honor of Clare of Rimini. Added in the second half of the sixteenth century. Incipit: *Hec est Christi pręelecta / Clara fide, clara vita.* Explicit: *Ne nostrarum sentiamus / Hunc culparum vindicem. Amen.*

Fol. iii^v: Copy of phrase found on a painting by Francesco Longhi, dedicated to Clare of Rimini, dated 1568. Added in the second half of sixteenth century: *Sopra l'ancona / Divę Clarę Ariminen' dicatum devotione quae tantam a Christo huc intrantibus exoravit indulgentiam.*

Ex-Libris Indications

Fol. 1^r: *Restitui debet monasterio S. Mariae de Angelis Arimin.* Related to the manuscript's loan to the Bollandist Daniel Papebroch (second half of seventeenth century).

Fol. i^v: *Questo libro è di me . . .* Ending obscured by ink spot (seventeenth century).

Fol. i^v: *Suor Elena Clementini, monaca nel convento degl'Angeli di Rimini* (seventeenth century).

Fol. 14^r: *Daniel Clemens Iuntii* (or *Nuntii*) (first half of sixteenth century).

Fol. 20^r: *Fr' Daniel* (same hand as previous notation).

Fol. iv^v: *In libro vechio inno righe 24 a carte 312 in tuto* (sixteenth century, related to text on fol. iii^{r–v}).

History

This manuscript was copied in the second half of the fifteenth century for the sisters of the community founded by Clare of Rimini, which took the name Santa Maria degli Angeli. It was given modest ornamentation in the early sixteenth century, about the time the community became a monastery of the Order of St. Clare. It remained at this community through the eighteenth century, except when it was transported to Anvers by the Bollandist Daniel Papebroch, presumably following his stay in Rimini in 1660. In 1810, the monastery of Santa Maria degli Angeli was destroyed. In 1880, the manuscript was held by the archives of the cathedral chapter of Rimini. These were absorbed into the collection of the Biblioteca del Seminario Vescovile (see A. Turchini, *Inventario dei mss. della Biblioteca del Seminario di Rimini* [Rimini, 1974]), where our manuscript has resided ever since.

NOTES

Chapter 1

The chapter titles are our additions. They are not found in the manuscript.

1. Today in Emilia-Romagna, province of Rimini.

2. Italian region centered in Ravenna, between the Adriatic Sea on the east and Emilia on the west.

3. Clare's parents here receive the titles *messere* (for Chiarello) and *madonna* (for Gaudiana). *Messere* (the form *mesere* is used in the manuscript) does not necessarily imply noble status, but our translation as "Sir" is intended to convey a level of respect equivalent to "Lady" for Chiarello's wife. Chiarello's name indicates that he was the son of Piero, who was the son of Zacheo.

4. This date is clearly an error. Clare actually must have been born around 1260. Perhaps the date might have been written in Roman numerals as "MCCL" (1250) and later miscopied as "MCCC" (1300).

5. Thus her mother died in the late 1260s, and her father had remarried by around 1270.

6. If Clare was born around 1260, she would have turned twenty-four around 1284.

7. These executions must have followed Malatesta of Verucchio's installation as *podestà* (governor of the town) in 1282.

8. Clare would have reached the age of thirty-four around 1294.

Chapter 2

1. Cf. Eph. 4:18. Where the Italian text clearly quotes directly from the Bible, we place the text in italics. When there is an apparent allusion to biblical text but without a direct quotation, we use the abbreviation "Cf." (short for the Latin *confer*, meaning "see by way of comparison").

2. I.e., the Franciscans, or "Lesser Brothers" (*Fratres Minores* in Latin, *Frati Minori* in the Italian here). This is the first indication of Clare's ties to the Franciscan Order.

3. Cf. Matt. 14:30.

4. Francis of Assisi (1181–1226), founder of the Franciscan Order. For the location of the Franciscan church in Rimini (San Francesco), see Map 2 (in Chap. 5).

5. Cf. 1 Cor. 13:13.

6. A religious habit is usually the dress adopted by members of a religious order. But here, it may be the habit or clothing of a penitent, as a sign of renouncing worldly values.

7. In Chap. 1, Clare is said to have made her second marriage at (or after) the age of twenty-four and to have remained in the marriage until age thirty-four. Here, she is said to

have been married for twelve years, up to age thirty-four, which would suggest that she made the marriage at age twenty-two.

8. Cf. Apoc. 1:13.

9. *Chiara, veramente chiara.* The Italian text frequently plays on *Chiara* (the woman's name, Clare) and *chiara*, the adjective meaning "clear" or "bright." The play on words was often used in reference to St. Clare of Assisi, and this passage seems to draw on phrases about her found in Thomas of Celano's *Vita prima* of St. Francis, Alexander IV's bull of canonization for Clare of Assisi (*Clara claris praeclara meritis*), and Celano's *Legenda sanctae Clarae*.

Chapter 3

1. Having embraced the religious dress of a penitent, she is no longer "Lady Clare" but "Sister Clare."

2. Cf. Matt. 3:2, 4:17 ("Do penance, for the Kingdom of Heaven is at hand"). See further the commentary to Chap. 6.

3. John 1:29.

4. Cf. Bonaventure, *Legenda maior* 14,4. This echo of the Franciscan theologian and Minister General Bonaventure's *Life* of Francis may be our first hint that the author of the *Life of Clare* is a Franciscan.

5. Cf. Isa. 52:7; Rom. 10:5.

6. Cf. Matt. 10:14; Mark 6:11; Luke 9:5, 10:11.

7. The equivalent in modern American weight is about twenty pounds.

8. This is the first time the author refers to "sisters," even though he has not yet traced Clare's story to the point where she forms a community.

9. If her conversion occurred around 1294 and at age thirty-four, eighteen more years would take Clare to 1312 and age fifty-two.

10. Gen. 18:5.

11. Cf. Ps. 43:26.

12. Next to this passage, the scribe has written the sign "C." See Chap. 4, par. 15, at n. 15, where the scribe sends readers back to this point in the text. The phrase "root of David" in Clare's cry for help refers to Apoc. 5:5 and 22:16, and perhaps also to a well-known prayer attributed to the Franciscan St. Anthony of Padua but attested in earlier liturgical sources (*Ecce Crucem Domini! Fugite partes adversae! Vicit Leo de tribu Juda, Radix David! Alleluia!*). The prayer's context related to a woman beset by a demon, and so may have been called to mind here by Clare's fight against demonic temptation.

13. The hagiographer is looking forward to the period when Clare will establish herself in a cell within the city walls of Rimini, explained in Chap. 5.

14. Cf. Matt. 11:30.

15. St. Martin's day is November 11. This Lent (also called the Lent of Advent) lasted until Christmas Eve.

16. Epiphany is January 6.

17. This passage comes from the Franciscan Rule, the *Regula bullata*, 3:6 ("during that holy Lent that begins at the Epiphany and lasts during the forty days which our Lord consecrated by his own fast"). This borrowing strongly indicates that the author is a Franciscan.

18. Pentecost is the seventh Sunday after Easter; Ascension is forty days after Easter.

19. St. John the Baptist's day is June 24; hence the vigil is June 23.

20. Cf. Matt. 4:2; Luke 4:2.

21. In Chap. 5, the hagiographer will explain more fully Clare's cell within the city wall.

22. The Italian word is *panigello* (or *pannicello*), which could refer to a cloth given to the nearest female relative of the deceased in funeral processions.

23. Cf. 1 Tim. 1:15.

24. Cf. Matt. 9:13.

25. Cf. Phil. 2:19.

26. Cf. Eph. 1:7.

27. "Nearly" thirty years from her conversion (around 1294) would indicate that Clare lived until at least about 1324, when she would have been about sixty-four.

28. The "Nativity" is Christmas. The octave (a week later) is therefore January 1.

29. Clare would have turned sixty around 1320.

Chapter 4

1. Urbino is about sixty kilometers (thirty-seven miles) south of Rimini. Clare's brother probably suffered this new exile in about 1295, when the Malatesta family consolidated power in Rimini.

2. Cf. Isa. 18:4.

3. Gregory the Great, *Moralia in Iob*, XV, 53.

4. The ambiguous concluding phrase of this sentence (*como una madonna de sua consuetudine tenere era usata*) is difficult to translate with confidence. It could also be interpreted as "in the same way she had the habit of keeping an image of the Madonna."

5. This anonymous canon (a member of the cathedral chapter, the clerical community that surrounds the bishop) is the first churchman in the text to be presented as Clare's spiritual adviser.

6. The canonical hour of matins was recited at about 3 AM.

7. The canonical hour of nones (the ninth hour of the day) was recited at about 3 PM. I.e., Clare would remain in the church from well before dawn into mid-afternoon.

8. Cf. 1 Cor. 13:13.

9. Exod. 20:15.

10. Exod. 20:7, 16.

11. Cf. Isa. 58:7.

12. Cf. Matt. 25: 36.

13. Cf. Matt. 10:8, 11:5; Luke 7:22.

14. Cf. Prov. 27:8.

15. In the ms., the scribe has written the sign "C," sending the reader back to the passage in Chap. 3, par. 8, at n. 12, where this sign is placed next to Clare's words: "Arise for me, Christ, and help me! Come to me, you who are the guardian of men, the root of David, Hallelujah!"

16. Although Dominic died on August 6, 1221, his feast day was celebrated on August 5 in Italy at this time (the Catholic Church has more recently moved the feast to August 8).

17. The Preaching Brothers are the Dominicans. San Cataldo, the church of the Dominican convent, was established in Rimini in 1254.

18. The unique manuscript actually reads "Drudula." But this seems to be the same woman as Clare's biological sister, who is called Druditia several times later in the *Life*. Very likely, "Drudula" (not otherwise attested as an Italian name) was simply a misreading by the

scribe the first time he encountered this name ("itia" and "ula" have the same number of vertical strokes of the quill).

19. Cf. John 29:34.

20. The first named churchman to appear in the text. Girolamo Fisici was later bishop of Rimini from 1323 to 1328. See par. 70 (Chap. 12).

Chapter 5

1. "Santa Maria at the Wall" (Santa Maria in Muro) was located near Clare's cell. Since 1265, it had housed Cistercian nuns who had fled Constantinople when the "Latins" who had conquered that city in 1204 were driven out by the Greeks. The aristocracy of the "Latin" empire had been French-speaking—hence the reference to "ladies from France."

2. Matt. 18:20.

3. See Chap. 5 (par. 20).

4. Cf. 1 Cor. 3:16–17.

5. Chap. 8 (par. 37) will return to this theme.

6. The Sisters of Begno were nuns of the Order of St. Clare who fled their monastery at Castelbegni (today part of the commune of Montecopiolo in Emilia-Romagna, province of Rimini) to shelter in Rimini from 1288 to 1306. Hence this episode dates from before 1306.

7. Dino de' Rossi was a nobleman who served as *podestà* of Padua in 1314; his sister married into the Malatesta clan. The fact that he is here called Clare's "relative" indicates her elevated social status.

8. Cf. Jth. 16:17.

9. Cf. 1 Cor. 1:31; 2 Cor. 10:17.

10. Cf. Rom. 8:4.

11. Matt. 10:20.

Chapter 6

1. The phrasing here inverts the meaning found in Prov. 3:12 and Apoc. 3:19 ("God chastises whom he loves").

2. Grammatically, the passage could indicate either Clare's perfection or God's.

3. The term "patarine" (*paterina* in the Italian text) originally referred to eleventh-century lay reformers in Milan, but by this period could refer to any kind of deviant or heretic.

4. Matt. 15:22.

5. Cf. 1 Cor. 1:31; 2 Cor. 10:17.

6. Cf. Matt. 27:54.

Chapter 7

1. Heb. 4:12.

2. Cf. 1 Cor. 15:40–49.

3. Cf. Apoc. 11:15.

4. This story is repeated and expanded in Chap. 10 (par. 47).

5. This "Lord Bolognino" is otherwise unknown. The Massa Trabaria is at the meeting point of Tuscany, Umbria, the March of Ancona, and the Romagna. It is not clear how Clare got to this region or why she was there.

6. The Italian is *cognoscente veramente Christo parlare in la sua lingua*, which could be translated in several ways: "through her tongue" (= through Clare's words), "in his (= Christ's) language," "in his (= Bolognino's) language (= vernacular Italian)."

7. I.e., on their way to Venice, where the Fèsta de ła Sènsa was (and is) held on Ascension Day, forty days after Easter.

8. Cf. Luke 20:21.

9. This story is repeated and expanded in Chap. 10 (par. 53).

10. Cf. Luke 15:11–32 (parable of the prodigal son).

Chapter 8

1. San Matteo was the church serving the female community of Humiliati in Rimini.

2. The coronation of the Virgin (Mary reigning in heaven with her son placing a crown on her head) was an increasingly popular visual motif in the thirteenth and fourteenth centuries.

3. The Assumption of Mary (Mary being taken to heaven bodily after her death) was often represented with the Virgin being supported by two angels. Similar iconography frequently characterizes images of the Ascension of Jesus (Jesus rising bodily from the tomb).

4. The reference is unclear but might perhaps be to the Virgin Mary or Mary Magdalene.

5. Cagli lies between Urbino and Gubbio.

6. The same phrase, *mirabile visione*, appears in Dante, *Vita Nova* XLII, but it seems unlikely that our author was drawing directly upon that text.

7. An image representing the Virgin "in majesty," as queen of heaven.

8. The chapter repeats themes evoked in par. 19 (Chap. 5) above.

9. Ps. 92:5.

10. This is almost exactly the same sentence as in par. 36 above: "God showed with a marvelous vision that he wanted to enlarge her narrow cell so that she could stay there with additional sisters." There may be an allusion to Francis of Assisi, who writes in his Testament (14): "And after the Lord gave me some brothers, no one showed me what I had to do, but the Most High Himself revealed to me that I should live according to the pattern of the Holy Gospel."

11. Apparently Lapo, mentioned in par. 36 above.

12. The only time Clare is thus designated in the text.

13. I.e., she purchased the house.

14. Presumably, the same person as Clare's biological sister, mentioned in par. 16 (Chap. 4).

Chapter 9

1. Cf. Luke 22:44.

2. Cf. John 19:1–37.

3. Events in the next paragraph can be dated to late 1306. If this scene took place on preceding Good Fridays, Clare's last "performance" would have been April 1, 1306.

4. The reference to Clare's "cell" indicates that she began this yearly ritual before the purchase of Lapo's "place." The subsequent reference to "sisters" indicates that the practice continued into the period in which her spiritual sisters gathered around her at the newly purchased house.

5. Napoleone Orsini (1263–1342) was from one of the most powerful families of Rome and was made a cardinal in 1288. He was papal legate for the March of Treviso (in the Veneto), the Romagna, and other areas of northern Italy from 1306 to 1308 and is known to have been in Rimini in December 1306. A precise date can therefore be assigned to his interaction with Clare. As a supporter of Angelo Clareno and Ubertino of Casale, Napoleone Orsini was linked to ardent advocates of Franciscan poverty, known as "Spiritual" Franciscans.

6. Matt. 15:14.

7. "Following the proper order" (*secondo el debito ordine*) should probably be understood as "according to the *ordo breviarii*"; i.e., the structure of the liturgical calendar and office in the breviary.

8. This is the first time Clare's spiritual sisters are invoked as witnesses.

9. Cf. Ezek. 21:15.

10. Cf. John 3:21.

11. Cf. Ecclus. 25:19.

12. Cf. 1 Cor. 31; 2 Cor. 10:17.

Chapter 10

1. The medieval Italian *religione*, like the Latin *religio*, means "form of religious life."

2. This community, which had been founded just outside the city walls of Rimini by 1270, housed sisters who followed the way of religious life established by Santuccia Carabotti of Gubbio (d. 1305), following the Benedictine Rule but dedicated to works of charity and begging for their own alms.

3. Cf. Matt. 19:21, 29.

4. Cf. Mark 1:40–42.

5. A shorter version of this episode has already been related in par. 31 (Chap. 7).

6. Squirrel fur, widely used to trim garments in the thirteenth and fourteenth centuries.

7. I.e., a hair shirt worn for ascetic purposes.

8. Cf. Clare's own conversion, related in par. 4 (Chap. 2).

9. His crime was probably forgery or bearing false witness, since the Rimini city statutes specified the loss of a hand as the penalty for these offenses.

10. The reference to plural ruling lords from the Malatesta family dates this episode to 1317–1326, when Ferrantino and Pandolfo Malatesta shared power.

11. Rimini to Assisi is a five- or six-day walk of some 170 kilometers (105 miles). Urbino would be a first stop, a two-day walk of some sixty kilometers (thirty-seven miles) from Rimini. Cagli is another thirty-five kilometers (twenty-two miles) down the road toward Assisi. Gubbio, in Umbria, is thirty kilometers (nineteen miles) farther. Among Clare's sisters are Benedetta of Cagli (par. 36 [Chap. 8]) and Viola of Gubbio (par. 60 [Chap. 12]).

12. Cf. Mark 1:40–42.

13. I.e., the author wants to say that these other witnesses would be worth quoting, too. A similar formulation is found in par. 43 (Chap. 9).

14. Baroncello (Comune di Mengara) is ten kilometers (six miles) past Gubbio; it is about another thirty-five kilometers (twenty-two miles) from Mengara to Assisi.

15. Luke 6:19.

16. The indulgence granted for those who would pray at the Portiuncula from the evening of August 1 through August 2. On the Portiuncula, see n. 20 below.

17. Cf. Ps. 24:1.

18. These are the only two Latin words in the text. Meaning "Lift up your hearts," they come from the opening dialogue to the preface that the priest recites after the offertory and before performing the consecration.

19. I.e., on August 2, Clare and her companions went down to the Portiuncula.

20. The Portiuncula, or St. Mary of the Angels (Santa Maria degli Angeli), was a half-ruined little church, about four kilometers (two and a half miles) outside Assisi, that had been restored by Francis of Assisi in 1208. Hence it was of great importance to Franciscans and to the memory of St. Francis.

21. Grammatically, "in front of her eyes" might be the more accurate translation for *inanzi a soi ochi*, but the context seems to demand that this takes place in front of all Clare's companions.

22. This story has already been referred to, in par. 34 (Chap. 7).

23. "Divine theology" may designate either Holy Scripture or the learned discourse constructed from Holy Scripture; i.e., the "science of God."

24. Clare did not simply "answer" queries, but rather she "resolved" (*resolvecte*) academic questions apparently posed in the scholastic manner, in which possible answers were presented on both sides of a disputed subject.

25. Luke 2:25.

26. Cf. Matt. 10:20.

27. The palm branch was a symbol of Christian victory, loosely of the spirit over the flesh but specifically of martyrdom.

28. Cf. Prov. 27:21; Wisd. 3:6.

29. Cf. Matt. 24:21.

30. Cf. Ezek. 22:25.

31. 1 Thess. 5:2.

32. The Italian is *indivinatrice*, from the Latin *divinatrix*, meaning a prophetess or woman who tells the future. In this period, the root-word had the strongly negative connotation of one who used illicit, magical, or demonic means in order to prophesy.

Chapter 11

1. See Chap. 5 (par. 19) above. This passage is indeed found on fol. 8 of the manuscript, so this reference must have been added by the scribe of our manuscript; it may, however, modify an indication included by the original author.

2. The two uses of "order," first as a verb (*ordinassero*) and then as a noun (*ordine*), suggest that this nascent rebellion had to do with the specific form of life that Clare imposed on her sisters. They had no fixed rule or canonical "order" but only Clare as "mother" and founder to set the terms of their lives as penitents.

3. The shift from the second-person plural/formal (*vostro*) to the second-person singular/familiar (*tua*) may reflect a distinction between Clare the founder and Clare the daily leader.

4. John 14:27.

5. The feast day of St. Leonard is November 6.

6. Clare's vision was probably inspired by the iconographic program in the Augustinian church in Rimini (this hypothesis was first presented by Jacques Dalarun in *Claire de Rimini: Entre sainteté et hérésie* [Paris: Éditions Payot & Rivages, 1999]). In turn, this scene inspired

the right panel of the "Triptych of Rimini," made c. 1330 and today in Ajaccio's Musée Fesch, and the slightly later copy today in the National Gallery in London.

7. See n. 6 above.

Chapter 12

1. The demons are thus *incubi* (demons in male form) rather than *succubae* (demons in female form).

2. Cf. Matt. 6:10.

3. The feast day of Mary Magdalene is July 22, so the vigil is July 21.

4. The feast of the conversion of St. Paul is January 25.

5. Cf. Matt. 4:2.

6. Cf. Matt. 26:39.

7. Cf. Matt. 27:46.

8. I.e., three days after the feast of the conversion of St. Paul, or January 28.

9. According to prevailing medieval theory, mirrors produced, rather than reflected, light rays.

10. Often, the medieval laity took only the wafer, with the wine reserved for the officiating priest. Here it appears that Clare took the wine as well. The reference to eleven years, if taken literally, should indicate that these events did not take place at the very end of Clare's life.

11. Cf. Apoc. 1:13–16. The resurrected Christ was often painted in this manner, although Clare's following statement of belief does not mention the Resurrection.

12. Cf. John 29:34.

13. Cf. Matt. 14:13–21; Mark 6:31–44; Luke 9:10–17; John 6:1–13.

14. December 13. The adverb *finalmente* seems to suggest that Clare's death is drawing near, but the text does not conclude with a true description of her deathbed.

15. Cf. Aelred of Rivaux, *De Jesu puero duodenni* (Geoffrey Webb and Adrian Walker, trans., *On Jesus at Twelve Years Old* [London: A.R. Mowbray, 1956]).

16. Again, evidence that Clare took the chalice as well as the wafer.

17. A passage such as this is not found in Jeremiah, but there are similarities with Amos 8:11, as well as with Apoc. 7:16–17.

18. The original text of the *Life* ends here, with no mention of Clare's death.

Epilogue

1. Jacques Dalarun's critical edition of the Italian text reads here *ad vita* but notes the possibility that the scribe may have intended *adiuta*. Upon consideration, we have chosen to follow the latter reading ("supported").

2. Luke 23:46.

3. Cf. Thomas of Celano's *Vita prima* ("First Life") of St. Francis, 112–113, describing reactions to Francis's death.

4. The paragraph was added to the ms. by a hand of the second half of the sixteenth century. It was thus probably absent from the exemplar copied by the fifteenth-century scribe. It appears below par. 71 in the ms., but a pair of linked marginal signs indicates that it was intended to be inserted following par. 70.

5. Although this paragraph was copied by the same fifteenth-century scribe who made the rest of the ms. (and thus is presented in the ms. as part of Chap. 12), it must be an addition to the text dating from well after Clare's death, which actually occurred around 1324–1329

(unless the confusion could again arise from a miscopying of Roman numerals: perhaps MCCCXXVI [1326] was miscopied as MCCCXLVI [1346]. In that case, the most likely date for Clare's death would be February 10, 1326.)

6. Cf. Tob. 4:11; Ecclus. 3:30; Dan. 4:24.

7. Cf. Matt. 16:19.

8. Matt. 13:46.

9. Cf. 2 Kings 4.

10. Cf. 1 Kings 17:10–16; Luke 4:26.

11. Cf. John 12:3.

12. Cf. Gen. 28:12.

13. Cf. John 19:23.

14. This episode was added to the ms. by a hand of the second half of the sixteenth century, written on the recto side of the second flyleaf (fol. ii^r).

BIBLIOGRAPHY AND SUGGESTIONS
FOR FURTHER READING

Editions of the *Life*

Giuseppe Garampi published the first edition of *The Life of the Blessed Clare of Rimini*, in *Memorie ecclesiastiche appartenenti all'istoria e al culto della B. Chiara di Rimini* (Rome: Pagliarini, 1755), which offers a massive, pioneering study of her life and cult. The modern edition, with full and updated study, is Jacques Dalarun, *Lapsus linguae: La légende de Claire de Rimini* (Spoleto: Centro Italiano di studi sull'alto Medioevo, 1994).

Studies on Clare of Rimini

Besides the two editions/studies listed above, the only previous book-length treatment of Clare's life is Jacques Dalarun, *Claire de Rimini: Entre sainteté et hérésie* (Paris: Éditions Payot & Rivages, 1999). Little previous English-language scholarship is devoted specifically to Clare, beyond Jacques Dalarun, "Gospel in Action: The Life of Clare of Rimini," *Franciscan Studies* 64 (2006): 179–215; Elisa Tosi Brandi, "The Challenges of Chiara da Rimini: From Deeds to Words," in *From Words to Deeds: The Effectiveness of Preaching in the Late Middle Ages*, ed. Maria Giuseppina Muzzarelli (Turnhout: Brepols, 2014), 99–116. Studies treating Clare in French and Italian include Jacques Dalarun, "La Scrittura alla lettera. Del pericolo di una lettura letterale della Bibbia (Matteo III, 2 e IV, 17)," *Studi medievali*, 3rd ser., 32 (1991): 659–683; Raffaele Argenziano, "'Sante vive' attrici protagoniste della Passione tra mimesi e ascesi: i casi di Chiara da Rimini (†1326), Caterina da Siena (†1380) e Colomba da Rieti (†1501)," in *Terra santa e sacri monti. Atti della giornata di studio Università Cattolica, Aula Pio XI, 25 novembre 1998*, ed. Maria Luisa Gatti Perer (Milan: Istituto per la Storia dell'Arte Lombarda—Università Cattolica del Sacro Cuore, 1999), 167–175; Elisa Tosi Brandi: "L'abito della beata Chiara da Rimini (1260–c. 1324/29)," in *Gli Agolanti e il Castello di Riccione*, ed. Rosita Copioli (Rimini: Guaraldi, 2003), 331–338; Tosi Brandi, "Chiara da Rimini: beata e donna difficile," *Il Carrobbio. Tradizioni, problemi, immagini dell'Emilia-Romagna* 35 (2008): 23–27; Paolo Golinelli, "Agiografia e culto dei santi a Rimini nel pieno e basso Medioevo," in *Storia della Chiesa riminese*, vol. 2, ed. Augusto Vasina (Villa Verucchio/Rimini: Pazzini/Guaraldi, 2011), 357–361 (in the same vol., Riccardo Parmeggiani mentions Clare in the context of the Franciscans of Rimini [290]); Dalarun, "Da Chiara d'Assisi a Chiara da Rimini," in *Femminile, plurale. IV Festival francescano, Rimini, 28–30 settembre 2012*, ed. Dino Dozzi (Villa Verucchio: Pazzini, 2012), 71–84; Dalarun, "Un Huron chez les mystiques," in *Existe-t-il une mystique au Moyen Âge? Actes du colloque international, organisé par l'Institut d'Études Médiévales et tenu à l'Institut Catholique de Paris les 30 novembre et 1 décembre 2017*, ed. Dominique Poirel (Turnhout: Brepols, 2021), 171–184; Dalarun, "*Questa è perfida paterina*: Claire de Rimini, entre sainteté et hérésie," in *Le discours mystique entre Moyen Âge et première modernité, III. L'institution à l'épreuve*, ed. Véronique Ferrer, Marie-Christine Gomez-Géraud, and Jean-René Valette (Paris: Honoré Champion, 2021), 137–162. Concerning the refined Italian vernacular used in the *Life*, Giulio Perticari, *Dell'amor patrio di Dante e del suo libro intorno il volgare eloquio* (Bologna: Tipografia Bortolotti e Felicini, 1824), 321–324.

Chapter 1

Philip J. Jones, *The Malatesta of Rimini and the Papal State: A Political History* (Cambridge: Cambridge University Press, 1974), provides an English-language account of the rise of the Malatesta. In Italian, see, more recently, Angelo Turchini, *I Malatesta: Signori di Rimini e Cesena* (Cesena: Il Ponte Vecchio, 2013). For an introduction to Italian cities in this era, see Daniel P. Waley and Trevor Dean, *Italian City Republics*, 4th ed. (New York: Routledge, 2013). On the birth of the Italian communes, Chris Wickham, *Sleepwalking into a New World: The Emergence of Italian City Communes in the Twelfth Century* (Princeton, NJ: Princeton University Press, 2015). For the religious landscape, Augustine Thompson, *Cities of God: The Religion of the Italian Communes, 1125–1325* (University Park: Pennsylvania State University Press, 2005). For war and peace, Katherine Ludwig Jansen, *Peace and Penance in Late Medieval Italy* (Princeton, NJ: Princeton University Press, 2018). Marco Bartoli comments on Clare's political role in "Politica e santità femminile tra XIII e XIV secolo: appunti per continuare la ricerca," in *Negotium fidei. Miscellanea di studi offerti a Mariano d'Alatri in occasione del suo 80° compleanno*, ed. Pietro Maranesi (Rome: Istituto Storico dei Cappuccini, 2002), 234–236.

Chapter 2

An up-to-date study of medieval marriage is Elisabeth van Houts, *Married Life in the Middle Ages, 900–1300* (Oxford: Oxford University Press, 2019). For medieval sexuality, Constance M. Furey, "Sexuality," in *The Cambridge Companion to Christian Mysticism*, ed. Amy Hollywood and Patricia Z. Beckman (Cambridge: Cambridge University Press, 2012), 328–340; Ruth Mazo Karras, *Sexuality in Medieval Europe: Doing unto Others*, 3rd ed. (New York: Routledge, 2017). On medieval sanctity generally, see André Vauchez, *Sainthood in the Middle Ages*, trans. Jean Birrell (Cambridge: Cambridge University Press, 1997). For Italian holy women (including Margherita of Cortona, Angela of Foligno, Michelina of Pesaro, Umiliana de' Cerchi, and Umiltà of Faenza), a good starting place in English is E. Ann Matter, "Italian Holy Women: A Survey," in *Medieval Holy Women in the Christian Tradition, c. 1100–c. 1500*, ed. Alastair Minnis and Rosalynn Voaden (Turnhout: Brepols, 2010), 529–555. See also John Coakley and E. Ann Matter, eds., *Creative Women in Medieval and Early Modern Italy: A Religious and Artistic Renaissance* (Philadelphia: University of Pennsylvania Press, 1994); Daniel Bornstein and Roberto Rusconi, eds., *Women and Religion in Medieval and Renaissance Italy* (Chicago: University of Chicago Press, 1996). In French, see Jacques Dalarun, "Hors des sentiers battus. Saintes femmes d'Italie aux XIIIᵉ–XIVᵉ siècles," in *Femmes: mariages-lignages, XIIᵉ–XIVᵉ siècles. Mélanges offert à Georges Duby*, ed. Jean Dufournet (Brussels: De Boeck-Wesmael, 1992), 79–102. In Italian, Daniel Bornstein and Roberto Rusconi, eds., *Mistiche e devote nell'Italia tardomedievale* (Naples: Liguori, 1992); *Vita religiosa al femminile [secoli XIII–XIV]: Pistoia, 19–21 maggio 2017* (Pistoia: Centro Italiano di Studi di Storia e d'Arte Pistoia, 2019) (brief mentions of Clare in notes on pp. 39 and 203). A recent study on laypeople as saints in Italy (with a chapter on Margherita of Cortona) is Mary Harvey Doyno, *The Lay Saint: Charity and Charismatic Authority in Medieval Italy, 1150–1350* (Ithaca, NY: Cornell University Press, 2019); see also Maiju Lehmijoki-Gardner, *Worldly Saints: Social Interaction of Dominican Penitent Women in Italy, 1200–1500* (Helsinki: Suomen Historiallinen Seura, 1999). Radegund and her legacy are studied in Jennifer C. Edwards, *Superior Women: Medieval Female Authority in Poitiers' Abbey of Sainte-Croix* (Oxford: Oxford University Press, 2019). Angela of Foligno's writings can be read in Paul LaChance, trans., *Angela of Foligno: Complete Works* (New York: Paulist, 1993). For Margherita of Cortona, see Thomas Renna, trans., *The Life and Miracles of Saint Margaret of Cortona (1247–1297)*, ed. Shannon Larson (St. Bonaventure, NY: Franciscan Institute, 2012). For more on Umiliana de' Cerchi, see Anna Benvenuti Papi, "Umiliana dei Cerchi: nascita di un culto nella Firenze del Duecento," *Studi Francescani* 77 (1980): 87–117. For Giotto in Rimini, see Jill Farquhar, "A Florentine in Romagna: Giotto and the Decoration of the Church of San Francesco, Rimini," in *Visible Exports/Imports: New Research on Medieval and Renaissance European Art and Culture*, ed. Emily Jane Anderson, Jill Farquhar, and John Richards (Newcastle upon Tyne, UK: Cambridge Scholars, 2012), 38–57 (mention of Clare, 47).

Chapter 3

Caroline Walker Bynum, *Holy Feast and Holy Fast: The Religious Significance of Food to Medieval Woman* (Berkeley: University of California Press, 1987), unpacks the meanings of medieval women's eating, fasting, and asceticism. See also Dyan Elliott, "Flesh and Spirit: The Female Body," in *Medieval Holy Women in the Christian Tradition, c. 1100–c. 1500*, ed. Minnis and Voaden, 13–46. On female penitents in Italy, see Anna Benvenuti Papi, *In castro poenitentiae. Santità e società femminile nell'Italia medievale* (Rome: Herder, 1990); for a broader introduction, Walter Simons, "On the Margins of Religious Life: Hermits and Recluses, Penitents and Tertiaries, Beguines and Beghards," in *The Cambridge History of Christianity*, vol. 4, *Christianity in Western Europe c. 1100–c. 1500*, ed. Miri Rubin and Walter Simons (Cambridge: Cambridge University Press, 2009), 311–323. A good introduction to the mendicant orders (Franciscans and Dominicans) is C. H. Lawrence, *The Friars: The Impact of the Early Mendicant Movement on Western Society*, rev. ed. (London: I. B. Tauris, 2013). For the desert fathers, see Benedicta Ward, ed. and trans., *The Desert Fathers: Sayings of the Early Christian Monks*, rev. ed. (London: Penguin Classics, 2003).

The passage from Angela of Foligno's "Memorial" ("After I am emptied of this love . . .") can be found in LaChance, trans., *Angela of Foligno: Complete Works*, 184.

Chapter 4

On exile as a recurring theme in Italian politics, see Christine Shaw, *The Politics of Exile in Renaissance Italy* (Cambridge: Cambridge University Press, 2000). On women and almsgiving, Giuliana Albini, "Pauperismo e solidarietà femminile nell'Italia settentrionale (secoli XIII–XIV)," *Storia delle Donne* 13 (2017): 103–126 (mention of Clare, 110–111).

Chapter 5

Anyone who has not read Virginia Woolf's *A Room of One's Own* (first published 1929) should do so immediately. For several different perspectives on Clare of Assisi, see Lezlie S. Knox, *Creating Clare of Assisi: Female Franciscan Identities in Later Medieval Italy* (Boston: Brill,

2008); Marco Guida, *Una leggenda in cerca d'autore. La Vita di santa Chiara di Assisi. Studio delle fonti e sinossi intertestuale* (Brussels: Société des Bollandistes, 2010); Catherine M. Mooney, *Clare of Assisi and the Thirteenth-Century Church: Religious Women, Rules, and Resistance* (Philadelphia: University of Pennsylvania Press, 2016); Margaret Carney, *Light of Assisi: The Story of Saint Clare* (Cincinnati: Franciscan Media, 2021). For the fluid institutional framework around Franciscan women, see Bert Roest, *Order and Disorder: The Poor Clares Between Foundation and Reform* (Leiden: Brill, 2013); Alison More, *Fictive Orders and Feminine Religious Identities* (Oxford: Oxford University Press, 2018). For women as teachers and preachers, see Alastair Minnis, "Religious Roles: Public and Private," in *Medieval Holy Women in the Christian Tradition, c. 1100–c. 1500*, ed. Minnis and Voaden, 47–81. Christina of Hane's *Vita* can be read in Racha Kirakosian, trans., *The Life of Christina of Hane* (New Haven, CT: Yale University Press, 2020). On Hildegard of Bingen, see Barbara Newman, *Sister of Wisdom: St. Hildegard's Theology of the Feminine, with a New Preface, Bibliography, and Discography* (Berkeley: University of California Press, 1998).

The passage from Angela of Foligno's "Instructions" ("Here is the most vile of women . . .") can be found in LaChance, trans., *Angela of Foligno: Complete Works*, 219–220.

Chapter 6

An excellent introduction to the subject is Jennifer Kolpacoff Deane, *A History of Medieval Heresy and Inquisition* (Lanham, MD: Rowman & Littlefield, 2011). For an update, see Jessalynn Lea Bird, "Recent Trends and Future Directions in the Study of Medieval Religion, Heresy and Inquisitions," *English Historical Review* 135 (2020): 1260–1286. For Italy specifically, see Jill Moore, *Inquisition and Its Organisation in Italy, 1250–1350* (York: York Medieval Press, 2019). On "Cathars," Antonio Sennis, ed., *Cathars in Question* (York: York Medieval Press, 2018). Janine Larmon Peterson, *Suspect Saints and Holy Heretics: Disputed Sanctity and Communal Identity in Late Medieval Italy* (Ithaca, NY: Cornell University Press, 2019), studies figures like Clare of Rimini (mentioned p. 38), who occupy the line between heresy and sanctity, as does Paolo Golinelli, "Da santi ad eretici. Culto dei santi e propaganda politica tra Due e Trecento," in *La propaganda politica nel basso medioevo. Atti del XXXVIII Convegno storico internazionale, Todi, 14–17 ottobre 2001* (Spoleto: Centro italiano di studi sull'alto Medioevo, 2002), 471–510 (discussion of Clare, 485–489). For more detail on Rimini, see Jacques Dalarun, "Hérésie, commune et inquisition à Rimini (fin XIIe–début XIVe siècle)," *Studi medievali*, 3rd ser., 29 (1988): 641–683, updated by several works by Riccardo Parmeggiani, including "Inquisizione e frati Minori in Romagna, Umbria e Marche nel Duecento," in *Frati Minori e inquisizione. Atti del XXXIII Convegno internazionale, Assisi, 6–8 ottobre 2005* (Spoleto: Centro Italiano di studi sull'alto Medioevo, 2006), 113–150; *I consilia procedurali per l'inquisizione medievale (1235–1330)* (Bologna: Bononia University Press, 2011); *Explicatio super officio inquisitionis. Origini e sviluppi della manualistica inquisitoriale tra Due e Trecento* (Rome: Edizioni di storia e letteratura, 2012). Zanchino Ugolini's work has recently been discussed in Peter Diehl, "An Inquisitor in Manuscript and in Print: The *Tractatus super materia hereticorum* of Zanchino Ugolini," in *The Book Unbound: Editing and Reading Medieval Manuscripts and Texts*, ed. Siân Echard and Stephen Partridge (Toronto: University of Toronto Press, 2004), 58–77; Lorenzo Paolini, in "L'eresia catara a Rimini (secoli XII–XIII)," in *Storia della Chiesa riminese*, vol. 2, ed. Augusto Vasina (Villa Verucchio/Rimini: Pazzini/Guaraldi, 2011), 293–315; Derek Hill, *Inquisition in the Fourteenth Century: The Manuals of Bernard Gui and Nicholas of Eymerich* (York: York Medieval Press, 2019). Bernard Gui's manual can be read in Janet Shirley, trans., *The Inquisitor's Guide: A Medieval Manual on Heretics* (Welwyn Garden City, UK: Ravenhall, 2006). On Segarelli and Dolcino, see Jerry B. Pierce, *Poverty, Heresy, and the Apocalypse: The Order of Apostles and Social Change in Medieval Italy 1260–1307* (London: Bloomsbury Academic, 2012). On the "demonological turning point," Alain Boureau, *Satan the Heretic: The Birth of Demonology in the Medieval West*, trans. Teresa Lavender Fagan (Chicago: University of Chicago Press, 2006).

The quotation from Monsignor Giacomo Villani ("All the houses and buildings of the patarines . . .") is from an unpublished ms.: Rimini, Biblioteca civica Gambalunga, SC-MS. 175, Giacomo Villani, *De vetusta Arimini urbe et eius episcopis*, vol. 2, fol. 106r.

Chapter 7

See David Burr, *The Spiritual Franciscans: From Protest to Persecution in the Century After Saint Francis* (University Park: Pennsylvania State University Press, 2001), with chap. 12 on Ubertino of Casale and chap. 13 on Angelo Clareno. More broadly on lay followers of the Spirituals, see Louisa A. Burnham, *So Great a Light, So Great a Smoke: The Beguin Heretics of Languedoc* (Ithaca, NY: Cornell University Press, 2008). On the idea of apostolicity applied to a woman, Karen Scott, "St. Catherine of Siena, 'Apostola,'" *Church History* 61 (1992): 34–46.

Chapter 8

For an introduction to the Humiliati, see Frances Andrews, *The Early Humiliati* (Cambridge: Cambridge University Press, 2000). For women specifically, Sally Mayall Brasher, *Women of the Humiliati: A Lay Religious Order in Medieval Civic Life* (New York: Routledge, 2003). A classic introduction to fourteenth-century saints is Richard Kieckhefer, *Unquiet Souls: Fourteenth-Century Saints and Their Religious Milieu* (Chicago: University of Chicago Press, 1984). For Margherita Colonna, see Larry F. Field, trans., *Visions of Sainthood in Medieval Rome: The Lives of Margherita Colonna by Giovanni Colonna and Stefania*, ed. Lezlie S. Knox and Sean L. Field (Notre Dame, IN: University of Notre Dame Press, 2017). For Francis of Assisi's struggles as a founder, see Jacques Dalarun, *Francis of Assisi and Power* (St. Bonaventure, NY: Franciscan Institute, 2007). More broadly on Francis, see André Vauchez, *Francis of Assisi: The Life and Afterlife of a Medieval Saint*, trans. Michael F. Cusato (New Haven, CT: Yale University Press, 2012), and for his own writings and the early writings about him, Regis J. Armstrong, J. A. Wayne Hellman, and William J. Short, eds. and trans., *Francis of Assisi: Early Documents*, vol. 1, *The Saint* (New York: New City Press, 2001). On women and religious space, see Adrian Randolph, "Regarding Women in Sacred Space," in *Picturing Women in Renaissance and Baroque Italy*, ed. Geraldine A. Johnson and Sara F. Matthews Grieco (Cambridge: Cambridge University Press, 1997), 17–41, 250–256; Anne Jacobson Schutte, Thomas J. Kuehn, and Silvana Seidel Manchi, eds., *Time, Space, and Women's Lives in Early Modern Europe* (Kirksville, MO: Truman State University Press, 2001); Catherine Lawless, "'Make Your House Like a Temple': Gender, Space, and Domestic Devotion in Medieval Florence," *Religions* 3 (2020): 1–22.

Chapter 9

The title of this chapter refers to Théophile Desbonnets's classic work *From Intuition to Institution: The Franciscans* (Chicago: Franciscan Herald Press, 1988). On flagellants and 1260, see

Piroska Nagy and Xavier Biron-Ouellet, "A Collective Emotion in Medieval Italy: The Flagellant Movement of 1260," *Emotion Review* 12 (2020): 135–145. On the links between Clare of Montefalco, Margherita of Cortona, Angela of Foligno, and the Spirituals (with some discussion of the understudied Napoleone Orsini), see Burr, *The Spiritual Franciscans*, appendix. For a series of essays on "the WomanChrist model," see Barbara Newman, *From Virile Woman to WomanChrist: Studies in Medieval Religion and Literature* (Philadelphia: University of Pennsylvania Press, 1995). Max Weber's work (first published in German, posthumously, in 1921) can be read as *Economy and Society,* ed. Guenther Roth and Claus Wittich, 2 vols. (Berkeley: University of California Press, 2013).

The quotation from the manuscript copy of the Statutes of the Commune of Rimini is edited in Jacques Dalarun, "Hérésie, commune et inquisition à Rimini (fin XIIᵉ–début XIVᵉ siècle)," *Studi medievali,* 3rd ser., 29 (1988): 680.

Chapter 10

Santuccia of Carabotti is treated in Katherine Gill, "Scandala: Controversies Concerning Clausura in Women's Religious Communities in Late Medieval Italy," in Scott L. Waugh and Peter D. Diehl, eds., *Christendom and Its Discontents: Exclusion, Persecution, and Rebellion, 1000–1500* (Cambridge: Cambridge University Press, 1996), 177–203. On Douceline of Digne, see Kathleen Garay and Madeleine Jeay, *The Life of Saint Douceline, Beguine of Provence* (Cambridge: D. S. Brewer, 2001); for the quotation ("Lady Douceline, what is the soul?"), see p. 55. On pilgrimage to Assisi, see Mario Sensi, *Il perdono di Assisi* (Assisi: Porziuncola, 2002) (mention of Clare, 153–154), and the essays in Stefano Brufani and Enrico Menestò, eds., *Assisi anno 1300* (Assisi: Porziuncola, 2002). The translation of *Cum quibusdam* ("women commonly known as beguines") is from Elizabeth Makowski, "When Is a Beguine Not a Beguine? Names, Norms, and Nuance in Canonical Literature," in *Labels and Libels: Naming Beguines in Northern Medieval Europe,* ed. Letha Böhringer, Jennifer Kolpacoff Deane, and Hildo van Engen (Turnhout: Brepols, 2014), 83–98. On Marguerite Porete and Margueronne of Bellevillette, see Sean L. Field, *Courting Sanctity: Holy Women and the Capetians* (Ithaca, NY: Cornell University Press, 2019), chap. 6.

Chapter 11

Good introductions to medieval visions are Steven F. Kruger, *Dreaming in the Middle Ages* (Cambridge: Cambridge University Press, 1992); Barbara Newman, "What Did It Mean to Say 'I Saw'? The Clash Between Theory and Practice in Medieval Visionary Culture," *Speculum* 80 (2005): 1–43. For an overview of dream interpretation in the Italian Middle Ages, see Valerio Cappozzo, *Dizionario dei sogni nel Medioevo. Il Somniale Danielis in manoscritti letterari* (Florence: Leo S. Olschki, 2018). For Francis's and Dominic's difficulties in 1220, see pt. 2 of Jacques Dalarun, *To Govern Is to Serve: An Essay on Medieval Democracy,* trans. Sean L. Field (Ithaca, NY: Cornell University Press, 2023). Dalarun first showed that Clare's vision must have been inspired by the images in the Augustinian church of Rimini, in *Claire de Rimini. Entre sainteté et hérésie* (Paris: Éditions Payot & Rivages, 1999). On these frescoes, see Francesco Filippini, "Gli affreschi nell'abside della chiesa di S. Agostino in Rimini e un ritratto di Dante," *Bollettino d'arte del Ministero della pubblica istruzione: notizie dei musei, delle gallerie e dei monumenti d'Italia* 15 (1921): 3–21; H. Beenken, "The Master of the 'Last Judgement' at Rimini," *Burlington Magazine* 67 (1935): 53–66; Angelo Turchini, Claudio Lugato, and

Alessandro Marchi, *Il Trecento riminese in Sant'Agostino a Rimini* (Cesena: Il Ponte Vecchio, 1995); Daniele Benati, ed., *Il Trecento riscoperto. Gli affreschi della chiesa di Sant'Agostino a Rimini* (Milan: Silvana editoriale, 2019). The pioneering work on the triptychs depicting Clare of Rimini is Federico Zeri, "The Triptychs of the Beata Chiara of Rimini," *Burlington Magazine* 92 (1950): 246–251. See also Dillian Gordon, "The Vision of the Blessed Clare of Rimini," *Apollo* 124 (1986): 150–153; Dominique Thiébaut, *Ajaccio, musée Fesch: Les Primitifs italiens* (Paris: Éditions de la Réunion des musées nationaux, 1987), 144–153; Pier Giorgio Pasini, *Arte e storia della Chiesa riminese* (Milan: Skira, 1999), 159–165; Michela Messina, "I due trittici della beata Chiara da Rimini," *Studi romagnoli* 51 (2000): 795–821. On the clothing of Franciscan penitents, see Joanna Cannon and André Vauchez, *Margherita of Cortona and the Lorenzetti: Sienese Art and the Cult of a Holy Woman in Medieval Tuscany* (University Park: Pennsylvania State University Press, 1999); more broadly, Cordelia Warr, *Dressing for Heaven: Religious Clothing in Italy, 1215–1545* (Manchester: Manchester University Press, 2010).

The quotation about Francis of Assisi ("And the Lord told me what He wanted . . ."), from "The Assisi Compilation," can be found in Regis J. Armstrong, J. A. Wayne Hellmann, and William J. Short, trans., *Francis of Assisi: Early Documents*, vol. 2, *The Founder* (New York: New City Press, 2000), 133.

Chapter 12

For Ermine of Reims as an extreme example of a medieval holy woman beset by demons, see Renate Blumenfeld-Kosinski, *The Strange Case of Ermine of Reims: A Medieval Woman Between Saints and Demons* (Philadelphia: University of Pennsylvania Press, 2015). On "spiritual" or "mystical" pregnancy, see Gábor Klaniczay, "The Mystical Pregnancy of Birgitta and the Invisible Stigmata of Catherine: Bodily Signs of Supernatural Communication in the Lives of Two Mystics," in *Sanctity and Female Authorship: Birgitta of Sweden & Catherine of Siena*, ed. Maria H. Oen and Unn Falkeid (New York: Routledge, 2020), 159–178; Barbara Newman, *The Permeable Self: Five Medieval Relationships* (Philadelphia: University of Pennsylvania Press, 2021), 185–201. Hadewijch's works can be read in Mother Columba Hart, trans., *Hadewijch: The Complete Works* (New York: Paulist, 1980). On Eucharistic devotion, see Miri Rubin, *Corpus Christi: The Eucharist in Late Medieval Culture* (Cambridge: Cambridge University Press, 1991); Caroline Walker Bynum, "Woman Mystics and Eucharistic Devotion in the Thirteenth Century," in *Fragmentation and Redemption: Essays on Gender and the Human Body in Medieval Religion* (New York: Zone, 1992), 119–150. For bleeding hosts and anti-Semitism, see Miri Rubin, *Gentile Tales: The Narrative Assault on Late Medieval Jews* (New Haven, CT: Yale University Press, 1999). On "discernment of spirits," see Rosalynn Voaden, *God's Words, Women's Voices: The Discernment of Spirits in the Writing of Late-Medieval Women Visionaries* (York: York Medieval Press, 1999); Nancy Caciola, *Discerning Spirits: Divine and Demonic Possession in the Middle Ages* (Ithaca, NY: Cornell University Press, 2003); Dyan Elliott, *Proving Woman: Female Spirituality and Inquisitorial Culture in the Later Middle Ages* (Princeton, NJ: Princeton University Press, 2004); Wendy Love Anderson, *The Discernment of Spirits: Assessing Visions and Visionaries in the Late Middle Ages* (Tübingen: Mohr Siebeck, 2011). Constance of Rabastens's visions can be read in *Two Women of the Great Schism: The Revelations of Constance de Rabastens by Raymond de Sabanac and Life of the Blessed Ursulina of Parma by Simone Zanacchi*, ed. and trans. Renate Blumenfeld-Kosinski and Bruce L. Venarde (Toronto: Iter, 2010).

Epilogue

For Simon of Rimini, see M.-H. Laurent, ed., "Legenda cuiusdam b. Symonis," in *Analecta bollandiana* 58 (1949): 44–47. On confessor/holy women pairs, see John W. Coakley, *Women, Men, and Spiritual Power: Female Saints and Their Male Collaborators* (New York: Columbia University Press, 2006). On Na Prous Boneta, see Burnham, *So Great a Light, So Great a Smoke*, chap. 4. Dante Alighieri's *Divine Comedy* (comprising *The Inferno, Purgatorio*, and *Paradiso*) can be read in Robert Hollander and Jean Hollander's translation (New York: Doubleday, 2000–2007); and his *De Vulgari Eloquentia* in a translation by Steven Botterill (Cambridge: Cambridge University Press, 2005). Good introductions to Dante include Robert Hollander, *Dante: A Life in Works* (New Haven, CT: Yale University Press, 2001); Guy P. Raffa, *The Complete Danteworlds: A Reader's Guide to the Divine Comedy* (Chicago: University of Chicago Press, 2009); Giuseppe Mazzotta, *Reading Dante* (New Haven, CT: Yale University Press, 2014). For Francis of Assisi's vernacular poetry, see Jacques Dalarun, *The Canticle of Brother Sun: Francis of Assisi Reconciled*, trans. Philippe Yates (St. Bonaventure, NY: Franciscan Institute, 2016). Clare's role as a preacher is noted in Beverly Mayne Kienzle and Travis Allen Stevens, "Preaching, Heresy, and the Writing of Female Hagiography," in *Beyond Catholicism: Heresy, Mysticism, and Apocalypse in Italian Culture*, ed. Fabrizio De Donno and Simon Gilson (New York: Palgrave Macmillan, 2014), 43–44.

On Clare's later cult and beatification process, see the two works by Garampi and Dalarun listed above under "editions"; the prologue to Dalarun, *Claire de Rimini. Entre sainteté et hérésie*; Dalarun, "La part du faux. Les bienheureux Andrea et Giovanni, franciscains de Rimini au XIVᵉ siècle," *Mélanges de l'École française de Rome: Moyen-Âge* 102 (1990): 79–129; Stefano De Carolis and Elisa Tosi Brandi, "Iano Planco, il cardinal Garampi ed un miracolo della beata Chiara da Rimini. Quando l'allievo supera il maestro," *Studi romagnoli* 51 (2000): 295–307; De Carolis, "Un pittore seicentesco ed una beata medievale: Angelo Sarzetti (1656–1700 c.) ed il 'corpo' della Beata Chiara da Rimini," in *Atti della XXXV Tornata dello Studio Firmano per a storia del l'arte medica et della scienze (Fermo, 4–6 maggio 2001)*, ed. Alfredo Serrani (Fermo: A. Livi, 2002), 69–75. The fifteenth-century manuscript of the *Vita* is mentioned in Donatella Frioli, "Il libro e il testo agiografico: l'esempio del patrimonio riminese," in *Storia della Chiesa riminese*, vol. 2, ed. Augusto Vasina (Villa Verucchio/Rimini: Pazzini/Guaraldi, 2011), 177–178. For a valiant attempt at defending an eighteenth-century Franciscan against charges of forgery, Francesco Costa, "La B. Chiara da Rimini (ca. 1260–1326) e le pretese falsificazioni di Francescantonio Righini OFM Conv (1722–1779)," *Miscellanea francescana* 101 (2001): 792–825. On the rediscovery and scientific examination of Clare's relics, Stefano De Carolis and Elisa Rastelli, "Il ritorno della Beata: la ricognizione delle reliquie di Chiara da Rimini," *Studi Romagnoli* 63 (2012): 843–855. A fascinating comparison of an Italian saint's cult over the long term is Lester K. Little, *Indispensable Immigrants: The Wine Porters of Northern Italy and Their Saint, 1200–1800* (Manchester: Manchester University Press, 2015). For a rejection of the idea of the medieval period as a "dark age," see Matthew Gabriele and David Perry, *The Bright Ages: A New History of Medieval Europe* (New York: HarperCollins, 2021).

INDEX

ACKNOWLEDGMENTS

We would like to thank Jerry Singerman and Ruth Mazo Karras for their early interest in this project, and Jenny Tan for her unflagging enthusiasm, her timely support, and her improving suggestions in guiding this book to publication with the University of Pennsylvania Press. Daniel Bornstein and an anonymous reader for the press offered much-appreciated corrections and suggestions, while Cecilia Gaposchkin generously lent her time and talents in crafting the maps.

This collaborative project is rooted in Jacques Dalarun's groundbreaking research on Clare of Rimini's life and *Life*, and some of the ideas that we develop here were first expressed in his 1999 French-language study *Claire de Rimini: Entre sainteté et hérésie*. We are grateful to Éditions Payot & Rivages for permission to draw on that work in developing our new analysis.

We express our gratitude to the libraries, archives, and museums that allowed us to reproduce manuscripts, paintings, and other images, especially the diocese of Rimini and its Archivio Storico, the Palais Fesch-Musée des Beaux-Arts d'Ajaccio, and the Silver Special Collections Library of the University of Vermont. We particularly thank Dr. Stefano De Carolis for permission to use his photograph of Clare's relics.

Sean Field thanks the Humanities Center at the University of Vermont for a fellowship in 2021 that provided time away from teaching in order to complete this project, and for a generous subvention that helped to cover the cost of the book's production.